collections

Close Reader

GRADE 8

Program Consultants:
Kylene Beers
Martha Hougen
Carol Jago
William L. McBride
Erik Palmer
Lydia Stack

Cover, Title Page Photo Credits: ©Tek Image/Getty Images

Printed in the U.S.A.

ISBN 978-0-544-08906-8

17 18 1468 20 19 18

4500707299 B C D E F G

COLLECTION **1**

Culture and Belonging

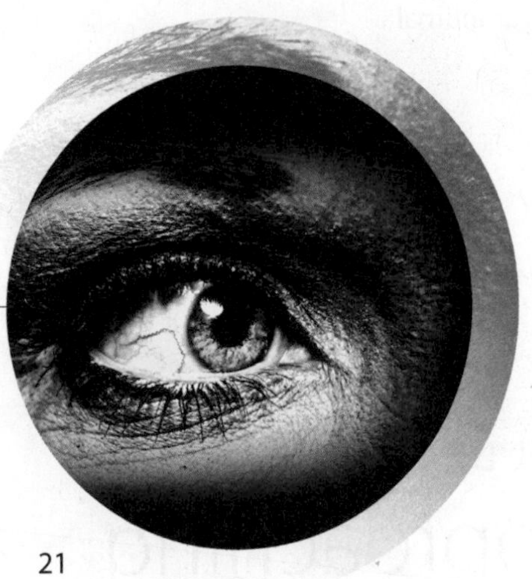

COLLECTION **2**

The Thrill of Horror

COLLECTION **3**
The Move Toward Freedom

COLLECTION **4**
Approaching Adulthood

COLLECTION 5
Anne Frank's Legacy

COLLECTION 6
The Value of Work

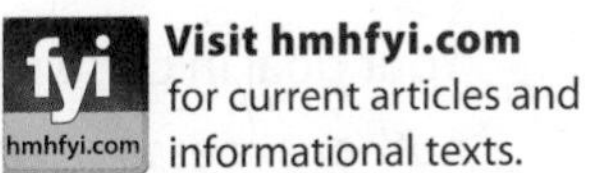

Visit hmhfyi.com for current articles and informational texts.

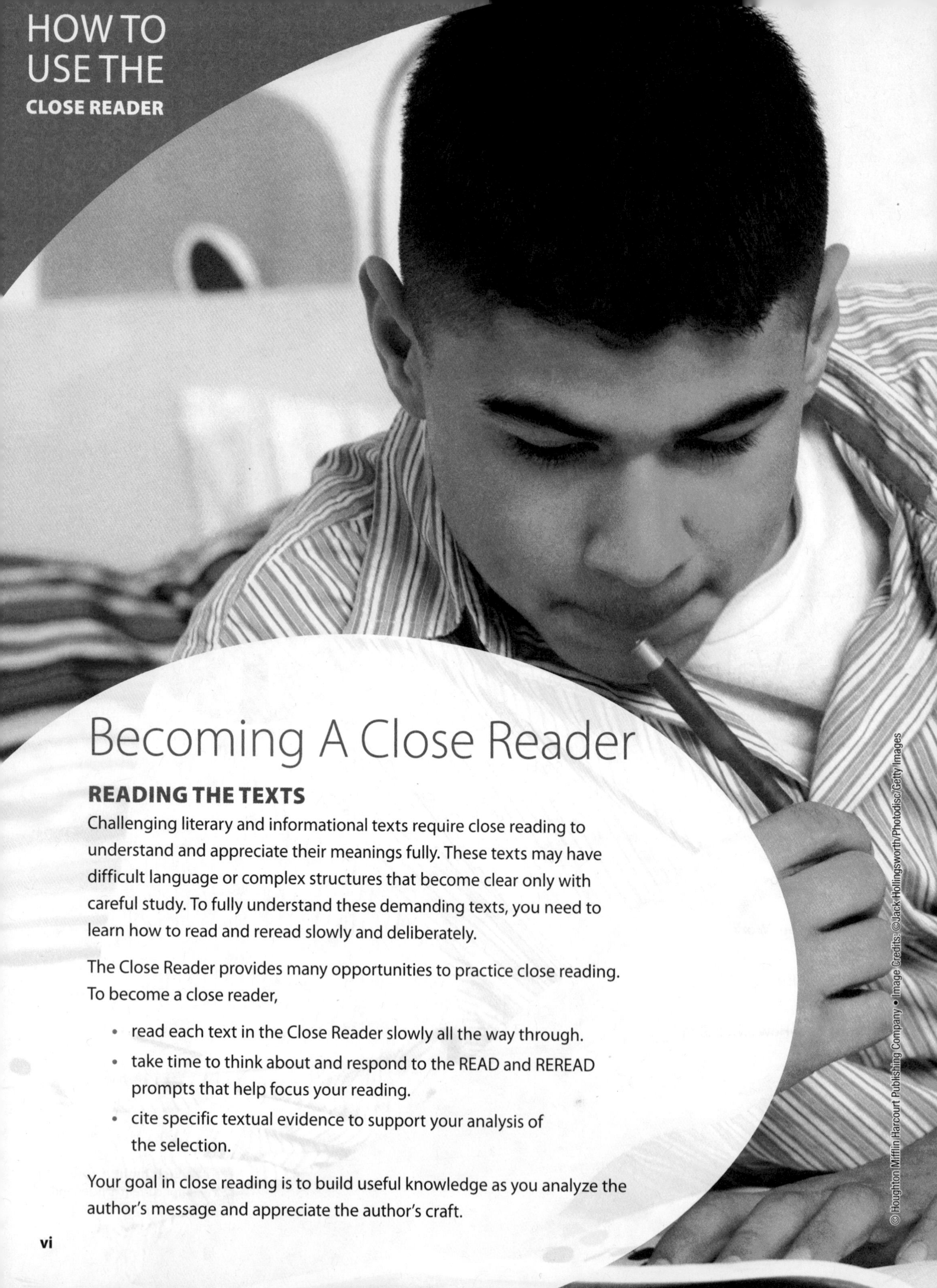

Becoming A Close Reader

READING THE TEXTS

Challenging literary and informational texts require close reading to understand and appreciate their meanings fully. These texts may have difficult language or complex structures that become clear only with careful study. To fully understand these demanding texts, you need to learn how to read and reread slowly and deliberately.

The Close Reader provides many opportunities to practice close reading. To become a close reader,

- read each text in the Close Reader slowly all the way through.
- take time to think about and respond to the READ and REREAD prompts that help focus your reading.
- cite specific textual evidence to support your analysis of the selection.

Your goal in close reading is to build useful knowledge as you analyze the author's message and appreciate the author's craft.

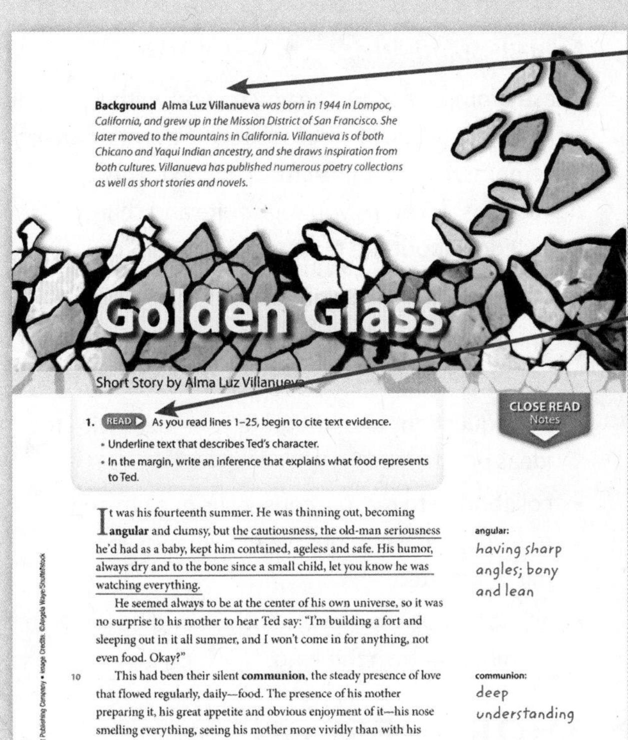

Background

This paragraph provides information about the text you are about to read. It helps you understand the context of the selection through additional information about the author, the subject, or the time period in which the text was written.

READ ▶

With practice, you can learn how to be a close reader. Questions and specific instructions at the beginning of the selection and on the bottom of the pages will guide your close reading of each text.

These questions and instructions

- refer to specific sections of the text.
- ask you to look for and mark up specific information in the text.
- prompt you to record inferences and text analysis in the side margins.
- help you begin to collect and cite text evidence.

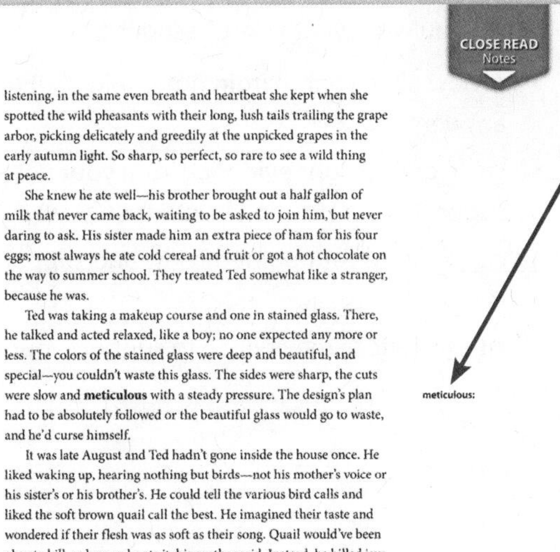

Vocabulary

Critical vocabulary words appear in the margin throughout most selections. Consult a print or online dictionary to define the word on your own.

When you see a vocabulary word in the margin,

- write the definition of each word in the margin.
- be sure your definition fits the context of the word as it is used in the text.
- check your definition by substituting it in place of the vocabulary word from the text. Your definition should make sense in the context of the selection.

◀ REREAD

To further guide your close reading, REREAD questions at the bottom of the page will

- ask you to focus on a close analysis of a smaller chunk of text.
- prompt you to analyze literary elements and devices, as well as the meaning and structure of informational text.
- help you go back into the text and "read between the lines" to uncover meanings and central ideas.

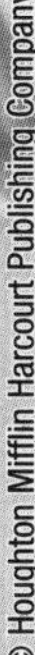

CLOSE READ Notes

The stained glass was finished and he decided to place it in his fort facing the back fields. In fact, it looked like the back fields—trees and the sun in a dark sky. During the day the glass sun shimmered a beautiful yellow, the blue a much better color than the sky outside: deeper, like night.

He was so used to sleeping outside now he didn't wake up during the night, just like in the house. One night, toward the end when he'd have to move back with everyone (school was starting, frost was coming and the rains), Ted woke up to see the stained glass full of light. The little sun was a golden moon and the inside glass sky and the outside sky matched.

In a few days he'd be inside, and he wouldn't mind at all.

10. REREAD AND DISCUSS Reread lines 136–147. With a small group, discuss what the stained glass means to Ted. Cite specific text evidence from the story in your discussion.

SHORT RESPONSE

Cite Text Evidence How does Ted change over the course of the summer? How does his relationship with his mother change? Review your reading notes, and be sure to **cite text evidence** from the story in your response.

8

REREAD AND DISCUSS

These prompts encourage you to work with a partner or in a small group to discuss specific events, details, statements, and evidence from the text. These discussions will allow you to acquire and share knowledge about the texts you are reading.

As you engage in these discussions,

- be sure to cite specific text evidence in support of your statements.
- pose questions and integrate your ideas with the ideas of others.
- collaborate to reach a consensus or call attention to evidence that might have been missed or misinterpreted.
- acknowledge the views of others and be ready to modify your own thinking.

SHORT RESPONSE

At the end of each text, you will have an opportunity to sum up your thinking by completing a Short Response. The Short Response represents a place to convey some of the ideas you have developed through close reading of the text.

When you write your Short Response,

- review all of your margin notes and REREAD answers.
- circle or highlight evidence from your notes that supports your position or point of view.
- clearly state your point of view and support it with reasons.
- cite specific text evidence to support your reasons.

COLLECTION **1**

Culture and Belonging

COLLECTION 1

Culture and Belonging

"Culture is the widening of the mind and of the spirit."

—Jawaharlal Nehru

Background **Alma Luz Villanueva** *was born in 1944 in Lompoc, California, and grew up in the Mission District of San Francisco. She later moved to the mountains in California. Villanueva is of both Chicano and Yaqui Indian ancestry, and she draws inspiration from both cultures. Villanueva has published numerous poetry collections as well as short stories and novels.*

Golden Glass

Short Story by Alma Luz Villanueva

CLOSE READ Notes

1. **READ ▶** As you read lines 1–25, begin to cite text evidence.
   - Underline text that describes Ted's character.
   - In the margin, write an inference that explains what food represents to Ted.

It was his fourteenth summer. He was thinning out, becoming **angular** and clumsy, but the cautiousness, the old-man seriousness he'd had as a baby, kept him contained, ageless and safe. His humor, always dry and to the bone since a small child, let you know he was watching everything.

angular:

He seemed always to be at the center of his own universe, so it was no surprise to his mother to hear Ted say: "I'm building a fort and sleeping out in it all summer, and I won't come in for anything, not even food. Okay?"

This had been their silent **communion**, the steady presence of love that flowed regularly, daily—food. The presence of his mother preparing it, his great appetite and obvious enjoyment of it—his nose smelling everything, seeing his mother more vividly than with his eyes.

communion:

He watched her now for signs of offense, alarm, and only saw interest. "Where will you put the fort?" Vida asked.

She trusted him to build well and not ruin things, but of course she had to know where. She looked at his dark, contained face and her eyes turned in and saw him when he was small, with curly golden hair, when he wrapped his arms around her neck. Their quiet times—undemanding—he could be let down, and a small toy could delight him for hours. She thought of the year he began kissing her elbow in passing, the way he preferred. Vida would touch his hair, his forehead, his shoulders—the body breathing out at the touch, his stillness. Then the explosion out the door told her he needed her touch, still.

"I'll build it by the redwoods, in the cypress trees. Okay?"

"Make sure you keep your nails together and don't dig into the trees. I'll be checking. If the trees get damaged, it'll have to come down."

"Jason already said he'd bring my food and stuff."

"Where do you plan to shower and go to the bathroom?" Vida wondered.

"With the hose when it's hot and I'll dig holes behind the barn," Ted said so quietly as to seem unspoken. He knew how to slither under her, smoothly, like silk.

"Sounds interesting, but it better stay clean—this place isn't that big. Also, on your dinner night, you can cook outdoors."

His eyes flashed, but he said, "Okay."

He began to gather wood from various stacks, drying it patiently from the long rains. He kept in his room one of the hammers and a supply of nails that he'd bought. It was early June and the seasonal creek was still running. It was pretty dark out there and he wondered if he'd meant what he'd said.

Ted hadn't seen his father in nearly four years, and he didn't miss him like you should a regular father, he thought. His father's image blurred with the memory of a football hitting him too hard, pointed (a bullet), right in the stomach, and the punishment for the penny candies—a test his father had set up for him to fail. His stomach

2. REREAD Reread lines 1–25. In the margin, write an inference about Ted's relationship with his mother, Vida.

3. READ As you read lines 26–59, underline text that suggests that Ted may change his mind about the fort.

hardened at the thought of his father, and he found he didn't miss him at all.

He began to look at the shapes of the trees, where the limbs were solid, where a space was provided (he knew his mother really would make him tear down the fort if he hurt the trees). The cypress was right next to the redwoods, making it seem very remote. Redwoods do that—they suck up sound and time and smell like another place. So he counted the footsteps, when no one was looking, from the fort to the house. He couldn't believe it was so close; it seemed so separate, alone—especially in the dark, when the only safe way of travel seemed flight (invisible at best).

Ted had seen his mother walk out to the bridge at night with a glass of wine, looking into the water, listening to it. He knew she loved to see the moon's reflection in the water. She'd pointed it out to him once by a river where they camped, her face full of longing—too naked somehow, he thought. Then, she swam out into the water, at night, as though trying to touch the moon. He wouldn't look at her. He sat and glared at the fire and roasted another marshmallow the way he liked it: bubbly, soft and brown (maybe six if he could get away with it). Then she'd be back, chilled and bright, and he was glad she went. Maybe I like the moon too, he thought, involuntarily, as though the thought weren't his own—but it was.

He built the ground floor directly on the earth, with a cover of old plywood, then scattered remnant rugs that he'd asked Vida to get for him. He **concocted** a latch and a door, with his hand ax over it, just in case. He brought his sleeping bag, some pillows, a transistor radio, some clothes, and moved in for the summer. The first week he slept with his buck knife open in his hand and his pellet gun loaded on the same side, his right. The second week Ted sheathed the knife and put it under his head, but kept the pellet gun loaded at all times. He

concocted

4. REREAD Reread lines 26–38. In the margin, write what you learn about Ted and Vida's relationship from the dialogue.

5. READ As you read lines 60–92, continue to cite textual evidence.

- Circle text that tells something Ted and Vida might have in common.
- In the margin, explain how the plot advances in each paragraph.

missed no one in the house but the dog, so he brought him into the cramped little space, enduring dog breath and farts because he missed *someone*.

Ted thought of when his father left, when they lived in the city, with forty kids on one side of the block and forty on the other. He remembered that one little kid with the funny sores on his body who chose an apple over candy every time. He worried they would starve or something worse. That time he woke up screaming in his room (he forgot why), and his sister began crying at the same time, "Someone's in here," as though they were having the same terrible dream. Vida ran in with a chair in one hand and a kitchen knife in the other, which frightened them even more. But when their mother realized it was only their hysteria, she became angry and left. Later they all laughed about this till they cried, including Vida, and things felt safer.

He began to build the top floor now but he had to prune some limbs out of the way. Well, that was okay as long as he was careful. So he stacked them to one side for kindling and began to brace things in place. It felt weird going up into the tree, not as safe as his small, contained place on the ground. He began to build it, thinking of light. He could bring his comic books, new ones, sit up straight, and eat snacks in the daytime. He would put in a side window facing the house to watch them, if he wanted, and a tunnel from the bottom floor to the top. Also, a ladder he'd found and repaired—he could pull it up and place it on hooks, out of reach. A hatch at the top of the ceiling for leaving or entering, tied down inside with a rope. He began to sleep up here, without the dog, with the tunnel closed off.

Vida noticed Ted had become cheerful and would stand next to her, to her left side, talking sometimes. But she realized she mustn't face him or he'd become silent and wander away. So she stood

6. **◀ REREAD AND DISCUSS** Reread lines 82–92. With a small group, discuss how Ted feels about his father leaving.

7. **READ ▶** As you read lines 93–135, continue to cite textual evidence.

- Underline text that shows that Ted has changed.
- In the margin, summarize how Ted has changed.
- In the margin, write something you learn about Ted when Vida compares him to wild pheasants in lines 107–112.

listening, in the same even breath and heartbeat she kept when she spotted the wild pheasants with their long, lush tails trailing the grape arbor, picking delicately and greedily at the unpicked grapes in the early autumn light. So sharp, so perfect, so rare to see a wild thing at peace.

She knew he ate well—his brother brought out a half gallon of milk that never came back, waiting to be asked to join him, but never daring to ask. His sister made him an extra piece of ham for his four eggs; most always he ate cold cereal and fruit or got a hot chocolate on the way to summer school. They treated Ted somewhat like a stranger, because he was.

Ted was taking a makeup course and one in stained glass. There, he talked and acted relaxed, like a boy; no one expected any more or less. The colors of the stained glass were deep and beautiful, and special—you couldn't waste this glass. The sides were sharp, the cuts were slow and **meticulous** with a steady pressure. The design's plan had to be absolutely followed or the beautiful glass would go to waste, and he'd curse himself.

meticulous:

It was late August and Ted hadn't gone inside the house once. He liked waking up, hearing nothing but birds—not his mother's voice or his sister's or his brother's. He could tell the various bird calls and liked the soft brown quail call the best. He imagined their taste and wondered if their flesh was as soft as their song. Quail would've been okay to kill, as long as he ate it, his mother said. Instead, he killed jays because they irritated him so much with their shrill cries. Besides, a neighbor paid Ted per bird because he didn't want them in his garden. But that was last summer and he didn't do that anymore, and the quail were proud and plump and swift, and Ted was glad.

8. **REREAD** Reread lines 119–125. Explain what Ted's attitude toward working with stained glass reveals about his character.

9. **READ** As you read lines 136–147, cite textual evidence.

- Underline text that describes the stained glass.
- In the margin, write an inference about why Ted "wouldn't mind at all" being inside again.

The stained glass was finished and he decided to place it in his fort facing the back fields. In fact, it looked like the back fields—trees and the sun in a dark sky. During the day the glass sun shimmered a beautiful yellow, the blue a much better color than the sky outside: deeper, like night.

He was so used to sleeping outside now he didn't wake up during the night, just like in the house. One night, toward the end when he'd have to move back with everyone (school was starting, frost was coming and the rains), Ted woke up to see the stained glass full of light. The little sun was a golden moon and the inside glass sky and the outside sky matched.

In a few days he'd be inside, and he wouldn't mind at all.

10. **REREAD AND DISCUSS** Reread lines 136–147. With a small group, discuss what the stained glass means to Ted. Cite specific text evidence from the story in your discussion.

SHORT RESPONSE

Cite Text Evidence How does Ted change over the course of the summer? How does his relationship with his mother change? Review your reading notes, and be sure to **cite text evidence** from the story in your response.

Background *The United States has always been a land of immigrants. During the 1600s and 1700s, fewer than one million people immigrated to the new country. Today, almost one million people immigrate to the United States each year, and those immigrants tend to be younger than the general population. They generally settle in areas where there are people with similar backgrounds. (This has always been true of immigrants to the United States.) Most immigrants today settle in one of seven states: California, New York, Florida, Texas, Pennsylvania, New Jersey, and Illinois.*

What to Bring

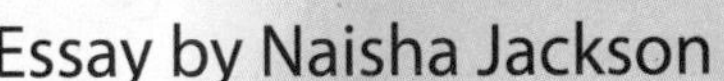

Essay by Naisha Jackson

CLOSE READ Notes

1. **READ ▶** As you read lines 1–24, begin to cite text evidence.
   - Circle the first subhead.
   - Underline the reasons people immigrate to the United States.
   - In the margin, list the items that immigrants have brought with them.

Traveling Light

A hundred years ago, most immigrants to the United States arrived by ship and were allowed only one suitcase for the long voyage. They left almost all of their belongings behind. Recent immigrants have a much faster journey, but many of them still bring very few items with them.

Some modern immigrants move to the United States to find a better future, owning very little in their countries of origin. One immigrant from Central Africa arrived at Kennedy Airport in 2002 with twenty cents—he worked in a car wash as he earned his college degree in finance. A man who emigrated from Honduras brought a ceramic Zorro pencil sharpener, which is now a treasured family possession.

Other immigrants are refugees, escaping **oppression** in their homelands. Many refugees are likely to have very few possessions, and are often unable to leave their countries with those belongings they do

oppression:

have. A man who was imprisoned for nine years in a Soviet political labor camp immigrated to the United States with the help of the International Organization for Migration. He arrived with only a small flight bag. One of the few items he had with him was a toothbrush he had kept in the labor camp, carved down so it could be hidden in his pocket from the guards. The thousands of children who left Cuba in 1960 were allowed to leave with only five dollars and a small suitcase. One child's suitcase held his bilingual edition of Shakespeare's *Hamlet*.

Precious Possessions

principles:

Are there any **principles** that guide what belongings an immigrant brings? There are requirements—legal documents such as passports and birth certificates—and there are items of choice. Some items you might expect, while others might come as a surprise to you.

Perhaps the two most common kinds of immigrants' belongings are religious items and photographs. Immigrants may have photographs of friends and relatives they are leaving and places they used to live. New arrivals have arrived with the following religious items in their luggage:

2. REREAD Reread lines 1–24. How does the subhead hint at the information in this section? Support your answer with explicit textual evidence.

3. READ As you read lines 25–56, continue to cite textual evidence.

- Underline the items that immigrants have brought with them.
- In the margin, note the categories the items fall into.

- a prayer book
- a Bible
- a Koran[1]
- a statue of Buddha[2]
- religious medals
- candlesticks for Sabbath candles

Immigrants often also bring things that will remind them of their homelands. A Chinese family brought ashes from the wood-burning stove they used to cook their last meal at home; a Greek woman brought a night-blooming jasmine plant. Gifts from friends also occupy space in their bags: a refugee family from violence in Ghana brought beaded necklaces they had been given. Along with a few documents, some photographs, and an x-ray proving that the father had been screened for tuberculosis, these were their only possessions.

Some people bring useful objects. A man who had worked casting metal escaped past armed Iron Curtain guards in Hungary with a small tool of his trade in his pocket. He started his own foundry in the United States, and still uses the tool—and he won't let anyone else use it! The husband of the woman with the night-blooming jasmine brought his barber's scissors with him, and started his shop at the local railway station. Many immigrant families bring cooking utensils—woks, rolling pins, stainless-steel bowls—and favorite knives.

[1] **Koran:** the sacred book of Islam that contains the revelations of God to Mohammad.
[2] **Buddha:** (563? – 483? B.C.), the founder of the religion of Buddhism.

4. **REREAD** Reread lines 29–39. Why might immigrants bring religious items and photographs with them? What does the bulleted list of items reveal about the variety of religious items brought? Support your answer with explicit textual evidence.

5. **READ** As you read lines 57–71, continue to cite textual evidence.

- Underline the items that immigrants have brought with them.
- In the margin, note the types of items mentioned in each paragraph.

Immigrants do not always know a lot about United States life; a Ukrainian family of refugees had four large duffel bags with them, packed tightly with bedding, which they had heard was expensive and inferior in America.

Sentimental Journeys

Remembrances of old lives take up immigrant suitcase space, too. Things that have been in the family for a long time help new arrivals feel more at home, or at least less alone. Parents' or grandparents' wedding rings are seldom neglected. Other items may not seem so valuable. A man who was a doctor in Myanmar brought his diploma, even though he cannot practice medicine in the United States. A girl from China brought her bright yellow metronome, simply because it was special—none of her friends had one—and she now finds that, unlike when she was in China, she enjoys practicing the piano.

And of course, young children (and some not so young) can be counted on to bring a favorite teddy bear.

6. **REREAD AND DISCUSS** Reread lines 1–71. With a small group, discuss the structure of the article. How might a circle graph or a bar graph add to the information given in the article?

SHORT RESPONSE

Cite Text Evidence What conclusions can you draw about the items immigrants chose to bring with them to the United States? **Cite text evidence** from the article in your response.

Background *A member of the Standing Rock Sioux,* **Susan Power** *was born in 1961 and grew up in Chicago. She spent her childhood listening to her mother tell stories about their American Indian heritage. These stories later served as inspiration for Power's writing. As a young girl, Power made frequent visits with her mother to local museums—trips that inspired her memoir "Museum Indians."*

Museum Indians

Memoir by Susan Power

1. READ ▶ As you read lines 1–16, begin to cite text evidence.
   - Underline a metaphor in the first paragraph that describes the mother's braid.
   - Underline a metaphor in the second paragraph that describes the mother's braid differently.
   - In the margin, note the adjectives the narrator uses to describe the braid.

A snake coils in my mother's dresser drawer; it is thick and black, glossy as sequins. My mother cut her hair several years ago, before I was born, but she kept one heavy braid. It is the three-foot snake I lift from its nest and handle as if it were alive.

"Mom, why did you cut your hair?" I ask. I am a little girl lifting a sleek black river into the light that streams through the kitchen window. Mom turns to me.

"It gave me headaches. Now put that away and wash your hands for lunch."

"You won't cut *my* hair, will you?" I'm sure this is a whine.

"No, just a little trim now and then to even the ends."

I return the dark snake to its nest among my mother's slips, arranging it so that its thin tail hides beneath the wide mouth sheared by scissors. My mother keeps her promise and lets my hair grow long, but I am only half of her; my thin brown braids will reach the middle of my back, and in maturity will look like tiny garden snakes.

My mother tells me stories every day: while she cleans, while she cooks, on our way to the library, standing in the checkout line at the supermarket. I like to share her stories with other people, and chatter like a monkey when I am able to command adult attention.

"She left the reservation when she was sixteen years old," I tell my audience. Sixteen sounds very old to me, but I always state the number because it seems integral to my recitation. "She had never been on a train before, or used a telephone. She left Standing Rock to take a job in Chicago so she could help out the family during the war. She was petrified of all the strange people and new surroundings; she stayed in her seat all the way from McLaughlin, South Dakota, to Chicago, Illinois, and didn't move once."

I usually laugh after saying this, because I cannot imagine my mother being afraid of anything. She is so tall, a true Dakota woman; she rises against the sun like a skyscraper, and when I draw her picture in my notebook, she takes up the entire page. She talks politics and attends sit-ins,[1] wrestles with the Chicago police and says what's on her mind.

[1] **sit-ins:** organized protest demonstrations in which participants seat themselves in appropriate places and refuse to move; the act of occupying the seats or an area of a segregated establishment to protest racial discimination.

2. **REREAD** Reread lines 12–16. Explain what the narrator means when she says "I am only half of her." Support your answer with explicit textual evidence.

3. **READ** As you read lines 17–34, continue to cite textual evidence.

- Underline a simile about the narrator, and in the margin, explain how it helps reveal the narrator's personality.
- Underline a simile about the mother, and in the margin, describe what it reveals about the narrator's view of her mother.

> **She is so tall, a true Dakota woman; she rises against the sun like a skyscraper. . . .**

I am her small shadow and witness. I am the timid daughter who can rage only on paper.

We don't have much money, but Mom takes me from one end of the city to the other on foot, on buses. I will grow up believing that Chicago belongs to me, because it was given to me by my mother. Nearly every week we tour the Historical Society, and Mom makes a point of complaining about the statue that depicts an Indian man about to kill a white woman and her children: "This is the only monument to the history of Indians in this area that you have on exhibit. It's a shame because it is completely one-sided. Children who see this will think this is what Indians are all about."

My mother lectures the guides and their bosses, until eventually that statue disappears.

Some days we haunt the Art Institute, and my mother pauses before a Picasso.[2]

"He did this during his blue period," she tells me.

I squint at the blue man holding a blue guitar. "Was he very sad?" I ask.

"Yes, I think he was." My mother takes my hand and looks away from the painting. I can see a story developing behind her eyes, and I tug on her arm to release the words. She will tell me why Picasso was blue, what his thoughts were as he painted this canvas. She relates anecdotes I will never find in books, never see footnoted in a

[2] **Picasso:** Pablo Picasso (1881–1973), Spanish artist whose work is some of the most influential in modern art.

4. **READ ▷** As you read lines 35–59, continue to cite textual evidence.

- Underline the text that reveals the mother's personality.
- Circle the text that reveals how the narrator sees herself.
- Make a note in the margin to explain the difference between the narrator and her mother.

biography of the master artist. I don't even bother to check these references because I like my mother's version best.

When Mom is down, we go to see the mummies at the Field Museum of Natural History. The Egyptian dead sleep in the basement, most of them still shrouded in their wrappings.

intrigue:

"These were people like us," my mother whispers. She pulls me into her waist. "They had dreams and **intrigues** and problems with their teeth. They thought their one particular life was of the utmost significance. And now, just *look* at them." My mother never fails to brighten. "So what's the use of worrying too hard or too long? Might as well be cheerful."

Before we leave this place, we always visit my great-grandmother's buckskin[3] dress. We mount the stairs and walk through the museum's main hall—past the dinosaur bones all strung together, and the stuffed elephants lifting their trunks in a mute trumpet.

disconcerting:

The clothed figures are **disconcerting** because they have no heads. I think of them as dead Indians. We reach the traditional outfits of the Sioux in the Plains Indian section, and there is the dress, as magnificent as I remembered. The yoke[4] is completely beaded—I know the garment must be heavy to wear. My great-grandmother

[3] **buckskin:** leather made from deerskin.
[4] **yoke:** a piece that supports the gathered parts of a garment.

5. REREAD Reread lines 51–59. What does the narrator mean when she says "I can see a story developing behind her eyes" (line 54)? Support your answer with explicit textual evidence.

6. READ Read lines 60–79, and underline text that reveals the mother's outlook on life.

used blue beads as a background for the geometrical design, and I point to the azure expanse.

"Was this her blue period?" I ask my mother. She hushes me unexpectedly, she will not play the game. I come to understand that this is a solemn call, and we stand before the glass case as we would before a grave.

"I don't know how this got out of the family," Mom murmurs. I feel helpless beside her, wishing I could reach through the glass to disrobe the headless mannequin. My mother belongs in a grand buckskin dress such as this, even though her hair is now too short to braid and has been trained to curl at the edges in a saucy flip.

We leave our fingerprints on the glass, two sets of hands at different heights pressing against the barrier. Mom is sad to leave.

"I hope she knows we visit her dress," my mother says.

There is a little buffalo across the hall, stuffed and staring. Mom doesn't always have the heart to greet him. Some days we slip out of the museum without finding his stall.

"You don't belong here," Mom tells him on those rare occasions when she feels she must pay her respects. "We honor you," she continues, "because you are a creature of great endurance and great generosity. You provided us with so many things that helped us to survive. It makes me angry to see you like this."

Few things can make my mother cry; the buffalo is one of them.

"I am just like you," she whispers. "I don't belong here either. We should be in the Dakotas, somewhere a little bit east of the Missouri River. This crazy city is not a fit home for buffalo or Dakotas."

7. **READ ▷** As you read lines 80–110, continue to cite textual evidence.

- Underline what the mother says to the buffalo, and explain what she means in the margin.
- Circle text that reveals the narrator's feelings about the city.

I take my mother's hand to hold her in place. I am a city child, nervous around livestock and lonely on the plains. I am afraid of a sky without light pollution—I never knew there could be so many stars. I lead my mother from the museum so she will forget the sense of loss. From the marble steps we can see Lake Shore Drive spill ahead of us, and I sweep my arm to the side as if I were responsible for this view. I introduce my mother to the city she gave me. I call her home.

8. **REREAD AND DISCUSS** Why does seeing the little buffalo make the mother cry? Discuss your thoughts with a partner.

SHORT RESPONSE

Cite Text Evidence Compare and contrast the personalities of the narrator and her mother. Review your reading notes, and be sure to **cite text evidence** in your response.

COLLECTION 2

The Thrill of Horror

COLLECTION **2**

The Thrill of Horror

"There is a . . . horror story that is only two sentences long: The last man on Earth sat alone in a room. There was a knock at the door."

—Frederick Brown

Background *"The oldest and strongest emotion of mankind is fear, and the oldest and strongest kind of fear is fear of the unknown." So says* **H. P. Lovecraft** *in the opening sentence of "Supernatural Horror in Literature," one of the best essays about horror fiction ever written. Plagued by nightmares and a fear of the unknown as a child, Lovecraft sought to exorcise his own fears by expressing them to his readers, believing that if his fears frightened him, they would terrify his audience.*

The Outsider

Short Story by H. P. Lovecraft

CLOSE READ Notes

1. **READ ▶** As you read lines 1–21, begin to collect and cite text evidence.
   - Circle the words that describe the narrator in lines 1–9.
   - Underline the words that describe the narrator's surroundings.
   - In the margin, write your impression of the narrator based on his description of himself and his surroundings.

Unhappy is he to whom the memories of childhood bring only fear and sadness. Wretched is he who looks back upon lone hours in vast and dismal chambers with brown hangings and maddening rows of antique books, or upon awed watches in twilight groves of grotesque, gigantic, and vine-encumbered trees that silently wave twisted branches far aloft. Such a lot the gods gave to me—to me, the dazed, the disappointed; the barren, the broken. And yet I am strangely content, and cling desperately to those sere memories, when my mind momentarily threatens to reach beyond to *the other*.

I know not where I was born, save that the castle was infinitely old and infinitely horrible; full of dark passages and having high ceilings where the eye could find only cobwebs and shadows. The stones in the crumbling corridors seemed always hideously damp, and there

accessible:

was an accursed smell everywhere, as of the piled-up corpses of dead generations. It was never light, so that I used sometimes to light candles and gaze steadily at them for relief; nor was there any sun outdoors, since the terrible trees grew high above the topmost **accessible** tower. There was one black tower which reached above the trees into the unknown outer sky, but that was partly ruined and could not be ascended save by a well-nigh impossible climb up the sheer wall, stone by stone.

I must have lived years in this place, but I cannot measure the time. Beings must have cared for my needs, yet I cannot recall any person except myself; or anything alive but the noiseless rats and bats and spiders. I think that whoever nursed me must have been shockingly aged, since my first conception of a living person was that of somebody mockingly like myself, yet distorted, shrivelled, and decaying like the castle. To me there was nothing grotesque in the bones and skeletons that strowed some of the stone crypts deep down among the foundations. I fantastically associated these things with every-day events, and thought them more natural than the coloured pictures of living beings which I found in many of the mouldy books. From such books I learned all that I know. No teacher urged or guided me, and I do not recall hearing any human voice in all those years—not even my own; for although I had read of speech, I had never thought to try to speak aloud. My aspect[1] was a matter equally unthought of, for there were no mirrors in the castle, and I merely regarded myself by instinct as akin to the youthful figures I saw

[1] **aspect:** facial expression or appearance.

2. REREAD Reread lines 10–21. In this paragraph, how do the narrator's statements about his background and his description of his surroundings create suspense? Support your answer with explicit textual evidence.

3. READ Read lines 22–40. Underline details about the narrator's upbringing that seem strange or unusual.

drawn and painted in the books. I felt conscious of youth because I remembered so little.

Outside, across the **putrid** moat and under the dark mute trees, I would often lie and dream for hours about what I read in the books; and would longingly picture myself amidst gay crowds in the sunny world beyond the endless forest. Once I tried to escape from the forest, but as I went farther from the castle the shade grew denser and the air more filled with brooding fear; so that I ran frantically back lest I lose my way in a labyrinth of nighted silence.

putrid:

So through endless twilights I dreamed and waited, though I knew not what I waited for. Then in the shadowy solitude my longing for light grew so frantic that I could rest no more, and I lifted entreating hands to the single black ruined tower that reached above the forest into the unknown outer sky. And at last I resolved to scale that tower, fall though I might; since it were better to glimpse the sky and perish, than to live without ever beholding day.

In the dank twilight I climbed the worn and aged stone stairs till I reached the level where they ceased, and thereafter clung perilously to small footholds leading upward. Ghastly and terrible was that dead, stairless cylinder of rock; black, ruined, and deserted, and sinister with startled bats whose wings made no noise. But more ghastly and terrible still was the slowness of my progress; for climb as I might, the darkness overhead grew no thinner, and a new chill as of haunted and venerable mould **assailed** me. I shivered as I wondered why I did not reach the light, and would have looked down had I dared. I fancied that night had come suddenly upon me, and vainly groped with one free hand for a window embrasure, that I might peer out and above, and try to judge the height I had attained.

assailed:

4. **◀ REREAD AND DISCUSS** Reread lines 22–40. Discuss with a small group whether the information the narrator shares about himself makes him seem more or less reliable. Cite details in your discussion.

5. **READ ▶** As you read lines 41–100, continue to cite text evidence.

- Underline the reason the narrator gives for attempting to escape from the castle, and restate it in the margin.
- Circle every use of the word *slab* in lines 67–83. In the margin, explain what image it calls to mind.
- Underline the text in lines 84–100 that describes where the narrator finds himself after scaling the tower.

> ***"Nothing I had before undergone could compare in terror with what I now saw . . ."***

All at once, after an infinity of awesome, sightless crawling up that concave and desperate precipice, I felt my head touch a solid thing, and I knew I must have gained the roof, or at least some kind of floor. In the darkness I raised my free hand and tested the barrier, finding it stone and immovable. Then came a deadly circuit of the tower, clinging to whatever holds the slimy wall could give; till finally my testing hand found the barrier yielding, and I turned upward again, pushing the slab or door with my head as I used both hands in my fearful ascent. There was no light revealed above, and as my hands went higher I knew that my climb was for the nonce ended; since the slab was the trap-door of an aperture leading to a level surface of greater circumference than the lower tower, no doubt the floor of some lofty and capacious observation chamber. I crawled through carefully, and tried to prevent the heavy slab from falling back into place, but failed in the latter attempt. As I lay exhausted on the stone floor I heard the eerie echoes of its fall, but hoped when necessary to pry it up again.

prodigious:

Believing I was now at a **prodigious** height, far above the accursed branches of the wood, I dragged myself up from the floor and fumbled about for windows, that I might look for the first time upon the sky, and the moon and stars of which I had read. But on every hand I was disappointed; since all that I found were vast shelves of marble, bearing odious oblong boxes of disturbing size. More and more I reflected, and wondered what hoary secrets might abide in this high apartment so many aeons cut off from the castle below. Then unexpectedly my hands came upon a doorway, where hung a portal of stone, rough with strange chiselling. Trying it, I found it locked; but with a supreme burst of strength I overcame all obstacles and dragged it open inward. As I did so there came to me the purest ecstasy I have ever known; for shining tranquilly through an ornate grating of iron, and down a short stone passageway of steps that ascended from the newly found doorway, was the radiant full moon, which I had never before seen save in dreams and in vague visions I dared not call memories.

Fancying now that I had attained the very **pinnacle** of the castle, I commenced to rush up the few steps beyond the door; but the sudden veiling of the moon by a cloud caused me to stumble, and I felt my way more slowly in the dark. It was still very dark when I reached the grating—which I tried carefully and found unlocked, but which I did not open for fear of falling from the amazing height to which I had climbed. Then the moon came out.

pinnacle:

Most daemoniacal of all shocks is that of the abysmally unexpected and grotesquely unbelievable. Nothing I had before undergone could compare in terror with what I now saw; with the bizarre marvels that sight implied. The sight itself was as simple as it was stupefying, for it was merely this: instead of a dizzying prospect of treetops seen from a lofty eminence, there stretched around me on the level through the grating nothing less than *the solid ground*, decked and diversified by marble slabs and columns, and overshadowed by an ancient stone church, whose ruined spire gleamed spectrally in the moonlight.

Half unconscious, I opened the grating and staggered out upon the white gravel path that stretched away in two directions. My mind, stunned and chaotic as it was, still held the frantic craving for light; and not even the fantastic wonder which had happened could stay my course. I neither knew nor cared whether my experience was insanity, dreaming, or magic; but was determined to gaze on brilliance and gaiety at any cost. I knew not who I was or what I was, or what my surroundings might be; though as I continued to stumble along I

6. ◀ **REREAD** Reread lines 67–100. What vivid words in the narrator's description of the tower climb create suspense?

7. **READ** ▶ As you read lines 101–133, continue to cite textual evidence.

- Underline text that creates suspense by building anticipation of events.
- Circle text that describes the narrator's confused mental state.
- In the margin, state how the narrator continues to build suspense.

became conscious of a kind of fearsome latent memory that made my progress not wholly fortuitous. I passed under an arch out of that region of slabs and columns, and wandered through the open country; sometimes following the visible road, but sometimes leaving it curiously to tread across meadows where only occasional ruins bespoke the ancient presence of a forgotten road. Once I swam across a swift river where crumbling, mossy masonry told of a bridge long vanished.

Over two hours must have passed before I reached what seemed to be my goal, a venerable ivied castle in a thickly wooded park; maddeningly familiar, yet full of perplexing strangeness to me. I saw that the moat was filled in, and that some of the well-known towers were demolished; whilst new wings existed to confuse the beholder. But what I observed with chief interest and delight were the open windows—gorgeously ablaze with light and sending forth sound of the gayest **revelry**. Advancing to one of these I looked in and saw an oddly dressed company indeed; making merry, and speaking brightly to one another. I had never, seemingly, heard human speech before;

revelry:

8. REREAD Reread lines 118–133. What impression do you form of the narrator's mental state? In what ways does his unreliability increase suspense? Cite explicit textual evidence in your answer.

9. READ As you read lines 134–160, continue to cite textual evidence.

- Circle each use of *I* in the text.
- Underline the narrator's contradictory statement in lines 134–138, and in the margin, paraphrase what he says.
- In lines 147–160, circle phrases that describe the actions of the partygoers.

and could guess only vaguely what was said. Some of the faces seemed to hold expressions that brought up incredibly remote recollections; others were utterly alien.

I now stepped through the low window into the brilliantly lighted room, stepping as I did so from my single bright moment of hope to my blackest convulsion of despair and realisation. The nightmare was quick to come; for as I entered, there occurred immediately one of the most terrifying demonstrations I had ever conceived. Scarcely had I crossed the sill when there descended upon the whole company a sudden and unheralded fear of hideous intensity, distorting every face and evoking the most horrible screams from nearly every throat. Flight was universal, and in the clamour and panic several fell in a swoon and were dragged away by their madly fleeing companions. Many covered their eyes with their hands, and plunged blindly and awkwardly in their race to escape; overturning furniture and stumbling against the walls before they managed to reach one of the many doors.

The cries were shocking; and as I stood in the brilliant apartment alone and dazed, listening to their vanishing echoes, I trembled at the thought of what might be lurking near me unseen. At a casual inspection the room seemed deserted, but when I moved toward one

10. REREAD Reread lines 147–160. Why does seeing the events in these lines from the narrator's point of view limit your understanding of what is actually happening? Support your answer with explicit textual evidence.

11. READ As you read lines 161–182, continue to cite textual evidence.

- Underline the text that describes the sound the narrator makes.
- In the margin, explain what causes him to make that sound.
- Circle vivid words and phrases that describe what the narrator sees.

of the alcoves I thought I detected a presence there—a hint of motion beyond the golden-arched doorway leading to another and somewhat similar room. As I approached the arch I began to perceive the presence more clearly; and then, with the first and last sound I ever uttered—a ghastly ululation[2] that revolted me almost as poignantly as its noxious cause—I beheld in full, frightful vividness the inconceivable, indescribable, and unmentionable monstrosity which had by its simple appearance changed a merry company to a herd of delirious fugitives.

I cannot even hint what it was like, for it was a compound of all that is unclean, uncanny, unwelcome, abnormal, and detestable. It was the ghoulish shade of decay, antiquity, and desolation; the putrid, dripping eidolon[3] of unwholesome revelation; the awful baring of that which the merciful earth should always hide. God knows it was not of this world—or no longer of this world—yet to my horror I saw in its eaten-away and bone-revealing outlines and leering, abhorrent **travesty** on the human shape; and in its mouldy, disintegrating apparel an unspeakable quality that chilled me even more.

travesty:

I was almost paralysed, but not too much so to make a feeble effort towards flight; a backward stumble which failed to break the spell in which the nameless, voiceless monster held me. My eyes bewitched by the glassy orbs which stared loathsomely into them, refused to close; though they were mercifully blurred, and shewed the terrible object but indistinctly after the first shock. I tried to raise my hand to shut out the sight, yet so stunned were my nerves that my

[2] **ululation:** howling or wailing.

[3] **eidolon:** phantom; image.

12. **◀ REREAD** Reread lines 174–182. In what way do the descriptions in these lines create suspense?

13. **READ ▶** Read lines 183–225. What has the narrator discovered about himself? What supernatural elements become clear in the story? Record your ideas in the margin. Continue to cite textual evidence.

> *I recognized, most terrible of all, the unholy abomination that stood leering before me . . .*

arm could not fully obey my will. The attempt, however, was enough to disturb my balance; so that I had to stagger forward several steps to avoid falling. As I did so I became suddenly and agonizingly aware of the *nearness* of the carrion[4] thing, whose hideous hollow breathing I half fancied I could hear. Nearly mad, I found myself yet able to throw out a hand to ward off the foetid apparition which pressed so close; when in one cataclysmic second of nightmarishness and hellish accident *my fingers touched the rotting outstretched paw of the monster beneath the golden arch.*

I did not shriek, but all the fiendish ghouls that ride the night-wind shrieked for me as in that same second there crashed down upon my mind a single fleeting avalanche of soul-annihilating memory. I knew in that second all that had been; I remembered beyond the frightful castle and the trees, and recognized the altered edifice in which I now stood; I recognized, most terrible of all, the unholy **abomination** that stood leering before me as I withdrew my sullied fingers from its own.

abomination:

But in the cosmos there is balm as well as bitterness, and that balm is nepenthe.[5] In the supreme horror of that second I forgot what had horrified me, and the burst of black memory vanished in a chaos of echoing images. In a dream I fled from that haunted and accursed pile, and ran swiftly and silently in the moonlight. When I returned to the churchyard place of marble and went down the steps I found the stone trap-door immovable; but I was not sorry, for I had hated the antique castle and the trees. Now I ride with the mocking and friendly ghouls on the night-wind, and play by day amongst the catacombs of Nephren-Ka[6] in the sealed and unknown valley of Hadoth[7] by the Nile. I know that light is not for me, save that of the

[4] **carrion:** decaying flesh.

[5] **nepenthe:** a drug mentioned in the *Odyssey* as a remedy for grief.

[6] **Nephren-Ka:** one of Lovecraft's mythical creations.

[7] **Hadoth:** one of Lovecraft's creations; a sealed valley by the Nile amid the hills of Neb that holds the catacombs of Nephren-Ka.

moon over the rock tombs of Neb, nor any gaiety save the unnamed feasts of Nitokris[8] beneath the Great Pyramid; yet in my new wildness and freedom I almost welcome the bitterness of alienage.

For although nepenthe has calmed me, I know always that I am an outsider; a stranger in this century and among those who are still men. This I have known ever since I stretched out my fingers to the abomination within that great gilded frame; stretched out my fingers and touched *a cold and unyielding surface of polished glass.*

---

[8] **Nitokris:** perhaps the last pharaoh of the Sixth Dynasty; she is used mythically in two of Lovecraft's stories.

14. **REREAD AND DISCUSS** Reread lines 221–225. With a small group, discuss whether you were surprised by the revelation at the end of the story. Cite explicit text evidence in your discussion.

SHORT RESPONSE

Cite Text Evidence Evaluate the narrator of "The Outsider." How credible is his presentation of events? Explain whether your understanding of the narrator added to the story's suspense. **Cite text evidence** in your response.

Background *This poem by* **Edward Field** *(born 1924) presents a new version of a famous character in literature, the monster brought to life by the scientist Dr. Frankenstein. In the original story by the English writer Mary Wollstonecraft Shelley, Dr. Frankenstein used portions of dead bodies to create a figure shaped like a man and then gave the creature the power to move and think by activating him with electricity.*

Frankenstein

Poem by Edward Field

1. **READ ▷** As you read lines 1–12, begin to collect and cite text evidence.
   - Underline details that describe the monster's appearance.
   - Circle the pronouns the speaker uses to refer to the monster.
   - In the margin, explain why the villagers think the monster is dangerous.

The monster has escaped from the dungeon
where he was kept by the Baron,
who made him with knobs sticking out from each side of his neck
where the head was attached to the body
and stitching all over
where parts of cadavers were sewed together.

He is pursued by the ignorant villagers,
who think he is evil and dangerous because he is ugly
and makes ugly noises.
They wave firebrands at him and cudgels and rakes,
but he escapes and comes to the thatched cottage
of an old blind man playing on the violin Mendelssohn's
"Spring Song."

Hearing him approach, the blind man welcomes him:
"Come in, my friend," and takes him by the arm.
"You must be weary," and sits him down inside the house.
For the blind man has long dreamed of having a friend
to share his lonely life.

The monster has never known kindness—the Baron was cruel—
but somehow he is able to accept it now,
and he really has no instincts to harm the old man,
for in spite of his awful looks he has a tender heart:
Who knows what cadaver that part of him came from?

The old man seats him at table, offers him bread,
and says, "Eat, my friend." The monster
rears back roaring in terror.
"No my friend, it is good. Eat—gooood"
and the old man shows him how to eat,
and reassured, the monster eats
and says, "Eat—gooood,"
trying out the words and finding them good too.

2. **REREAD** Reread lines 7–12. Does the speaker share the villagers' view that the monster is evil and dangerous? Support your answer with explicit textual evidence.

3. **READ** As you read lines 13–30, continue to cite textual evidence.

- Circle details that suggest the blind man's kindness to the monster.
- Underline phrases that describe the monster's personality.
- In the margin, write the reason the monster "rears back roaring in terror" (line 25).

The old man offers him a glass of wine,
"Drink, my friend. Drink—good."
The monster drinks, slurping horribly, and says,
"Drink—goood," in his deep nutty voice
and smiles maybe for the first time in his life.

Then the blind man puts a cigar in the monster's mouth
and lights a large wooden match that flares up in his face.
The monster, remembering the torches of the villagers,
recoils, grunting in terror.
"No, my friend, smoke—goood,"
and the old man demonstrates with his own cigar.
The monster takes a tentative puff
and smiles hugely, saying, "Smoke—goood,"
and sits back like a banker, grunting and puffing.

Now the old man plays Mendelssohn's "Spring Song" on the violin
while tears come into our dear monster's eyes
as he thinks of the stones of the mob, the pleasures of mealtime,
the magic new words he has learned
and above all of the friend he has found.

4. **REREAD** Reread lines 13–30. Explain why the old man is quick to welcome the monster into his house. Support your answer with explicit textual evidence.

5. **READ** As you read lines 31–55, cite additional textual evidence.

- Circle actions by the old man that are similar to those he has made before.
- Underline details that reveal how happy the monster is.
- In the margin, restate what will happen to the monster when the mob finds him.

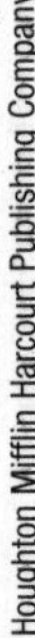

It is just as well that he is unaware—
being simple enough to believe only in the present—
that the mob will find him and pursue him
for the rest of his short unnatural life,
until trapped at the whirlpool's edge
he plunges to his death.

6. REREAD AND DISCUSS Reread lines 31–55. With a small group, discuss whether the time spent with the blind musician ultimately brought the monster more joy or more pain.

SHORT RESPONSE

Cite Text Evidence "We should not judge people by their appearance" is one of the themes of "Frankenstein." How do the events in the story and the characters' behavior convey this? **Cite text evidence** from the text to support your claims.

Background **Daniel Cohen** *has created over one hundred books for young readers on topics like sports, nature, history, and science fiction. In this essay, Cohen examines the Frankenstein monster. Mary Wollstonecraft Shelley, the monster's creator, began writing* Frankenstein: Or, The Modern Prometheus *in 1818 when she was only 18 years old. Frankenstein's monster has gone on to become an icon of popular culture. His image can be seen in movies, cartoons, and even cereal boxes.*

Man-Made Monsters

Essay by Daniel Cohen

1. READ ▶ As you read lines 1–19, begin to collect and cite text evidence.
   - Underline adjectives used to describe the scientist and the sorcerer.
   - Circle what the scientist and the sorcerer are seeking to acquire.
   - In the margin, restate what you learn about Prometheus.

With the publication of Mary W. Shelley's novel, *Frankenstein: Or, The Modern Prometheus*, in 1818, the mad scientist replaced the evil sorcerer as the master of monsters. In many respects the mad scientist and the evil **sorcerer** were very similar. They were not necessarily either mad or evil, at least not at first. Often they were brilliant, selfless, and dedicated to the task of acquiring knowledge—for the sorcerer magical knowledge, for the scientist scientific knowledge—that might benefit the human race.

sorcerer:

But the knowledge they sought was forbidden to mankind. Often for the best of motives, both sorcerer and scientist released great evil upon the world, and their knowledge ultimately destroyed them. That is why Mrs. Shelley chose the subtitle, *Or, the Modern Prometheus*, for her book. Prometheus was one of the Titans of Greek mythology. He was supposed to have given the human race the knowledge of fire, but this gift angered the gods and they punished him savagely.

CLOSE READ
Notes

Mary Shelley's scientist, Baron Victor von Frankenstein, attempted something no medieval sorcerer, no matter how powerful, could even aspire to—he sought to create life. Thus, Dr. Frankenstein's creation is the first truly modern monster in fiction.

According to tradition, the idea of the Frankenstein monster was first put into words in Switzerland on a stormy evening in 1816. A group of friends decided to pass the evening by telling stories based on supernatural events. Among those attending this storytelling session were two English poets, Lord Byron and Percy Bysshe Shelley. Also in attendance were Shelley's wife, Mary, and Byron's personal physician and friend, Dr. John Polidori. Dr. Polidori was reported to have told the tale of Lord Ruthven, who was to become the first famous vampire in English fiction. But surely the high point of the evening must have been Mary Shelley's story of Dr. Frankenstein and his creation.

There had never been anything quite like the Frankenstein monster in legend or fiction, but there were a few creatures the monster might have counted among its ancestors. One was Talus, a sort of ancient robot of Greek mythology. Talus was said to have been made of brass by Hephaestus, a god of fire and craftsmen. The job of the brass man was to protect the island of Crete. He drove off strangers by throwing rocks at them, or by heating himself red-hot and clasping the intruders in a lethal bear hug. Talus was animated by a single vein of blood running from his head to his foot, where it was closed with a nail. The powerful sorceress Medea put Talus to sleep and then cut the vein, allowing the vital fluid to pour out—thus killing the brass man.

2. **REREAD** Reread lines 9–19. In what way is Dr. Frankenstein similar to Prometheus?

3. **READ** As you read lines 20–49, continue to cite textual evidence.

- Circle the names of the mythical creatures mentioned in lines 31–49.
- Underline a description of each creature.
- In the margin, describe the duty each mythical creature was supposed to perform.

Somewhat closer to the Frankenstein monster was the golem, a creature of medieval Jewish legend. It was a clay figure said to be given life by some sort of magical charm. According to the legends, golems had been created by several famous medieval European rabbis. The golem was supposed to be a servant and protector of the Jews but it was untrustworthy. Rabbi Low, of sixteenth-century Prague,[1] had to destroy the golem he created when it went berserk.

Frankenstein's castle was located in the hills above the picturesque Bavarian city of Ingolstadt. Some have **speculated** that the inspiration for the Frankenstein story may have come from a German legend. There is a ruined castle outside of Frankfurt am Main, Germany, that contains the tomb of a medieval knight. This knight was supposed to have been killed by a ferocious man-eating, man-made monster that resembled a wild boar. But the legend itself is not at all clear and there is no way of knowing if this story or anything like it was ever encountered by Mary Shelley, although she was known to have traveled extensively in Europe.

speculate:

More likely Mrs. Shelley drew her inspiration for the story of Frankenstein from events of her own time. Science was becoming ever more important and it increasingly clashed with established beliefs and values. Frankenstein put life back into a creature that had been assembled from the limbs and organs of cadavers.[2]

[1] **Prague:** the capital and largest city of the Czech Republic.
[2] **cadaver:** a dead human body.

4. REREAD Reread lines 31–49. What is the writer's purpose for including the information on the Talus and the golem?

5. READ As you read lines 50–84, continue to cite textual evidence.

- Circle what the author believes inspired Mary Shelley to write her story.
- Underline reasons why body snatching was a flourishing trade in the eighteenth and nineteenth centuries.

During the eighteenth and much of the nineteenth centuries human bodies were not readily available for scientific study. Dissection of a corpse was considered both irreligious and illegal. The result was that doctors who wished to study the human anatomy had to employ the services of body snatchers who would exhume[3] newly buried corpses or cut down the hanging corpses of executed criminals and deliver them in secret to the laboratories. (While doctors couldn't dissect a body legally, it was considered perfectly proper to leave the corpse of a hanged man swinging until it rotted, as an example to other potential wrongdoers.)

Interest in medical science had grown enormously while the laws concerning dissection had not kept pace, so the body snatchers (the Resurrectionists or Sack-em-up Men as they were called in England) had a flourishing trade. If an adequate supply of corpses was unavailable, some of the more enterprising body snatchers would murder some unfortunates in order to sell their bodies. The most **notorious** of these murderers were Burke and Hare, who operated in Edinburgh, Scotland, at about the time that *Frankenstein* was written. The practice was fairly common throughout Europe, and many respectable doctors simply closed their eyes to what was happening.

notorious:

[3] **exhume:** to dig out from the ground.

6. REREAD Reread lines 60–84. How did the act of body snatching influence the writing of *Frankenstein*? Support your answer with explicit textual evidence.

7. READ As you read lines 85–102, continue to cite textual evidence.

- Circle phrases used to describe Frankenstein's monster in Mary Shelley's book.
- Underline phrases used to describe Frankenstein's monster in the 1931 film *Frankenstein*.
- In the margin, write one similarity between the monster in Shelley's book and the monster in the film *Frankenstein*.

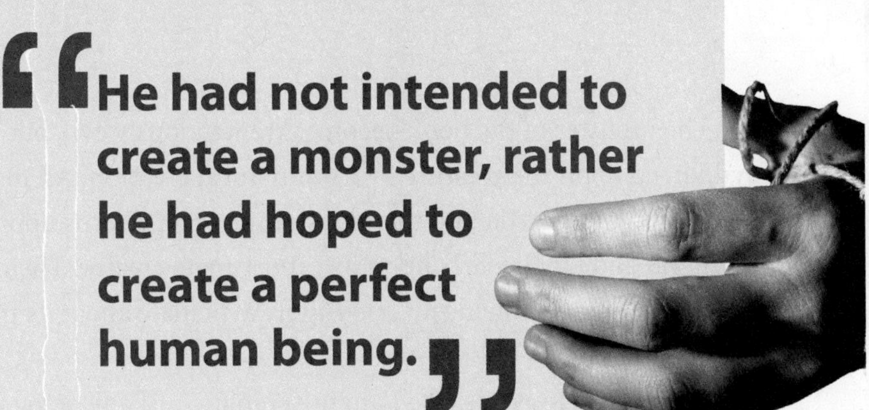

Dr. Frankenstein himself was forced to steal bodies for his experiments, and this was the first step in his crime. He had not intended to create a monster, rather he had hoped to create a perfect human being. But from the moment the creature opened its "dull yellow eye," the young scientist was overcome with disgust and horror. He realized that he had made an abomination, not a superman.

The monster in Mary Shelley's book is described as being exceptionally tall, yellow-eyed, and having skin like parchment. But few picture the Frankenstein monster as looking like that. Our image was fixed in 1931 with the appearance of the movie *Frankenstein*, starring a then unknown actor named Boris Karloff as the monster. Karloff's monster was a masterpiece of horrific makeup. It had a flat head and the overhanging brows of a Neanderthal man. Its face was crisscrossed with crude stitching, and two electrodes[4] stuck out of its neck. Like Mary Shelley's monster, the movie monster was unnaturally tall, but it also wore enormous leaden shoes and walked in a stiff, almost mechanical way.

[4] **electrode:** a conductor used to establish electrical contact with a non-metallic surface.

8. **REREAD AND DISCUSS** Reread lines 91–102. In a small group, discuss the differences between the monster's appearance in the book *Frankenstein* and its appearance in the movie *Frankenstein*.

9. **READ** As you read lines 103–120, continue to cite evidence.
   - Underline phrases that describe the temperament of the monster in Mary Shelley's book.
   - Circle phrases that describe the temperament of Frankenstein's monster in movies.
   - In the margin, explain what would need to happen for the monster in Mary Shelley's book to stop being miserable.

The monster of the book becomes tremendously evil, but it is an evil forced upon the creature by its unnatural creation. All mankind flees from it in horror, and the monster in revenge turns upon mankind and particularly upon its unfortunate creator. The monster of the book is also intelligent and highly articulate about its plight. At one point it says:

malicious:

"I am **malicious** because I am miserable. . . . If any being felt emotions of benevolence toward me, I should return them an hundred and an hundred fold. For that one creature's sake, I would make peace with the whole kind!"

The first of the long series of Frankenstein films simplified Mrs. Shelley's plot but retained much of the sympathy toward the monster. However, the creature's intelligence is largely lost in the films. Instead of making long, soul-searching speeches, the monster can only mumble and grunt. In later films the monster loses even this rudimentary speaking ability. It is reduced to a stiff, stumbling, and thoroughly evil automaton, more of a mechanical man than anything else.

10. **REREAD AND DISCUSS** Reread lines 113–120. With a small group, discuss why filmmakers do not emphasize the monster's intelligence. What effect might this have on viewers' perception of the monster?

SHORT RESPONSE

Cite Text Evidence Summarize what you learn about Mary Shelley's creation of Frankenstein's monster and the way the monster has been perceived since its creation. Review your reading notes, and **cite text evidence** of Mary Shelley's inspiration in the selection.

COLLECTION 3

The Move Toward Freedom

COLLECTION **3**

The Move Toward Freedom

"I should fight for liberty as long as my strength lasted."

—Harriet Tubman

BIOGRAPHY

My Friend Douglass — **Russell Freedman**

SHORT STORY

A Mystery of Heroism — **Stephen Crane**

JOURNAL ENTRIES

Civil War Journal — **Louisa May Alcott**

Background *In his book* Abraham Lincoln and Frederick Douglass: The Story Behind an American Friendship, **Russell Freedman** *reveals the unique friendship that developed between two men who only met three times. Both men were born poor, self-educated, and rose to prominence, one as the sixteenth President of the United States and the other as a powerful orator and influential abolitionist. In "My Friend Douglass," Freedman writes about what happened when Lincoln and Douglass met at the White House in 1865.*

My Friend Douglass

Biography by Russell Freedman

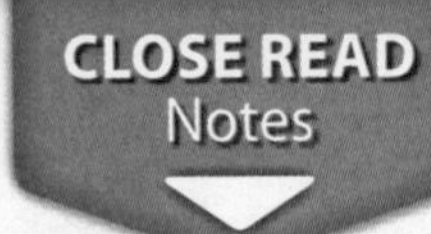

1. READ ▷ As you read lines 1–23, begin to cite text evidence.
   - Underline the date, the place, the name of the person involved in the action, and the historical event in lines 1–9.
   - In the margin, restate what Lincoln says that slavery has caused.
   - In lines 14–23, underline what Lincoln says will be an effect of the end of slavery.

On the morning of March 4, 1865, Frederick Douglass joined a festive crowd of 30,000 spectators at the U.S. Capitol to witness Abraham Lincoln's second **inauguration**. Weeks of rain had turned Washington's unpaved streets into a sea of mud, but despite the wet and windy weather, the crowd was in a mood to celebrate. Union troops were marching victoriously through the South. Everyone knew that the war was almost over. When Lincoln's tall figure appeared, "cheer upon cheer arose, bands blatted upon the air, and flags waved all over the scene."

inauguration:

Douglass found a place for himself directly in front of the speaker's stand. He could see every crease in Lincoln's careworn face as the president stepped forward to deliver his second inaugural address.

The Civil War had cost more than 600,000 American lives. The fighting had been more bitter and lasted far longer than anyone could

have imagined. The "cause of the war" was slavery, Lincoln declared. Slavery was the one institution that divided the nation. And slavery was a hateful and evil practice—a sin in the sight of God. "This mighty scourge of war" was a terrible retribution, a punishment for allowing human bondage to flourish on the nation's soil. Now that slavery was abolished, the time had come "to bind up the nation's wounds" and "cherish a just and lasting peace among ourselves and with all nations."

Following the "wonderfully quiet, earnest, and solemn" ceremony, Douglass wanted to congratulate Lincoln personally. That evening he joined the crowd heading to attend the gala inaugural reception at the White House—a building completed with slave labor just a half century earlier. "Though no colored persons had ever ventured to present themselves on such occasions," Douglass wrote, "it seemed, now that freedom had become the law of the republic, and colored men were on the battlefield, mingling their blood with that of white men in one common effort to save the country, that it was not too great an assumption for a colored man to offer his congratulations to the President with those of other citizens."

At the White House door, Douglass was stopped by two policemen who "took me rudely by the arm and ordered me to stand

2. REREAD Reread lines 14–23. If slavery was the "cause of the war," what were the effects of slavery? Be sure to cite explicit textual evidence in your response.

3. READ As you read lines 24–62, continue to collect and cite textual evidence.

- Circle the reason Douglass feels justified in attending the inaugural gala.
- Explain in the margin what happens when Douglass tries to enter the White House.
- Underline what Lincoln says to Douglass in lines 47–62.

back." Their orders, they told him, were "to admit no persons of my color." Douglass didn't believe them. He was positive that no such order could have come from the president.

The police tried to steer Douglass away from the doorway and out a side exit. He refused to leave. "I shall not go out of this building till I see President Lincoln," he insisted. Just then he spotted an acquaintance who was entering the building and asked him to send word "to Mr. Lincoln that Frederick Douglass is detained by officers at the door." Within moments, Douglass was being escorted into the elegant East Room of the White House.

Lincoln stood among his guests "like a mountain pine high above all others." As Douglass approached through the crowd, Lincoln called out, "Here comes my friend Douglass." The president took Douglass by the hand. "I am glad to see you," he said. "I saw you in the crowd today, listening to my inaugural address. How did you like it?"

Douglass hesitated. "Mr. Lincoln, I must not detain you with my poor opinion when there are thousands waiting to shake hands with you."

"No, no" said the president. "You must stop a little Douglass; there is no man whose opinion I value more than yours. I want to know what you think of it."

"Mr. Lincoln, that was a sacred effort," Douglass replied.

"I'm glad you liked it!"

And with that, Douglass moved on, making way for other guests who were waiting to shake the hand of Abraham Lincoln.

4. **REREAD** Reread lines 47–62. Explain how Lincoln makes Douglass feel welcome. Cite specific textual evidence in your response.

A month later, on April 9, 1865, generals Grant and Lee met at Appomattox Courthouse in Virginia, where Grant accepted the surrender of Lee's Confederate army. After almost four years of savage fighting, the Civil War had ended. "Guns are firing, bells ringing, flags flying, men laughing, children cheering, all, all **jubilant**," Gideon Welles, Lincoln's secretary of the navy, recorded in his diary.

jubilant:

Throngs of people collected around the White House, calling for the president. When Lincoln appeared, he asked the band to play "Dixie," a popular minstrel tune that had become associated with the Confederate cause. "It is one of the best tunes I have ever heard," Lincoln told the crowd. He joked that the tune was now "a lawful prize," since "we fairly captured it." So the band played "Dixie," then struck up "Yankee Doodle."

Five days later, as Lincoln sat watching a play with his wife at Ford's Theater in Washington, the president was shot in the head by actor John Wilkes Booth. Lincoln died early the next morning, April 15, 1865.

"A dreadful disaster has befallen the nation," Frederick Douglass told a memorial service in Rochester that afternoon. "It is a day for silence and meditation; for grief and tears."

For Douglass, Lincoln's death was "a personal as well as a national **calamity**." He felt that he had lost a friend, and how deeply he mourned that day for Abraham Lincoln, "I dare not attempt to tell. It was only a few days ago that I shook his brave, honest hand, and looked into his gentle eye and heard his kindly voice."

calamity:

5. READ ▷ As you read lines 63–87, continue to cite textual evidence.

- Circle words that indicate the sequence of events. List the events in the margin.
- Underline Douglass's response to the news of Lincoln's death.

6. ◁ REREAD Reread lines 80–87. In what way is Lincoln's death a "calamity" for Douglass? In what way is it a calamity for the nation?

A few months later Douglass received in the mail a long, slender package from Washington, D.C., along with a note from Mary Todd Lincoln. Her husband had considered Douglass a special friend, she wrote, and before he died, he had wanted to do something to express his warm personal regard. Since he hadn't had the chance, Mary had decided to send Douglass her husband's favorite walking stick as a memento of their friendship.

When Abraham Lincoln was assassinated, Frederick Douglass, in his mid-forties, was America's most influential black citizen. For the rest of his long life, he continued in his speeches and writings to be a powerful voice for social justice, denouncing racism and demanding equal rights for blacks and whites alike. During the Reconstruction era[1] of the 1870s and 1880s, when many of the rights gained after **emancipation** were snatched away in the South, Douglass spoke out against lynchings, the terrorism of the Ku Klux Klan, and the Jim Crow laws[2] that were devised to keep blacks in their place and away from the ballot box.

emancipation:

As he traveled widely, lecturing on social issues and national politics, Douglass spoke often about Abraham Lincoln. During the war, he had criticized the president for being slow to move against slavery, for resisting the enlistment of black soldiers, for inviting blacks "to leave the land in which we were born." But with emancipation, and in the aftermath of the war, Douglass had come to appreciate Lincoln's sensitivity to popular opinion and to admire the political skills Lincoln employed to win public support. "His greatest mission was to accomplish two things: first, to save the country from dismemberment and ruin; and, second, to free his country from the great crime of slavery. To do one or the other, or both," Douglass said, Lincoln needed "the earnest sympathy and the powerful cooperation of his fellow countrymen."

In the 1870s, Douglass moved with his family to Washington, D.C., where he edited a newspaper, held a succession of federal

[1] **Reconstruction era:** the period after the American Civil War when the Southern states were under the federal government's control.

[2] **Jim Crow laws:** the practice of separating African Americans from whites in the South during and after Reconstruction.

7. READ ▷ Read lines 88–139. In the margin, paraphrase what Douglass says about Lincoln in lines 112–117. Continue to cite evidence.

appointments, and clearly enjoyed his exalted position as an elder statesman of America's black citizens. And he continued to denounce injustice and inequality with the undiminished fervor of an old warrior.

His last home was a large, comfortable house called Cedar Hill, perched high on a hilltop looking down at the Anacostia River and the U.S. capital beyond. Cedar Hill had a spacious library, large enough to hold Douglass's collection of some two thousand books. From time to time, as he picked a book from his shelves and settled down to read, he must have recalled those distant days in Baltimore when he was a young slave named Frederick Bailey, a determined boy who owned just one book, a single volume that he kept hidden from view and read in secret.

Lincoln had read and studied the same book as a young man in New Salem. That was something they had in common, a shared experience that helped each of them rise from obscurity to greatness. "He was the architect of his own fortune, a self-made man," Douglass wrote of Lincoln. He had "ascended high, but with hard hands and honest work built the ladder on which he climbed"—words that Douglass, as he was aware, could easily have applied to himself.

8. **REREAD AND DISCUSS** Reread lines 128–135. With a small group, discuss the author's purpose for including the information about the shared book. What point is Freedman making about a childhood experience common to both men?

SHORT RESPONSE

Cite Text Evidence What effect did Lincoln have on Douglass's life? In what respect did Douglass carry on Lincoln's work? **Cite text evidence** in your response.

Background *Born in November of 1871,* **Stephen Crane** *began writing at the age of four.* The Red Badge of Courage, *his famous novel on the Civil War, was published when he was only twenty-four years old. The book made Crane a celebrity and national expert on the war. Crane interviewed Civil War veterans for his fictional writing, but they seemed unable to articulate their feelings about the war. As a result, Crane drew on his own imagination to fill in their thoughts and feelings to give his words larger meaning.*

A Mystery of Heroism

Short Story by Stephen Crane

CLOSE READ Notes

1. **READ ▷** As you read lines 1–23, begin to cite text evidence.
   - Underline details that reveal the setting, time, and place the action occurs. Write the setting in the margin.
   - Circle images that appeal to your sense of sight, smell, or hearing.
   - In the margin, restate what Fred Collins says in lines 13–15.

The dark uniforms of the men were so coated with dust from the incessant wrestling of the two armies that the regiment almost seemed a part of the clay bank which shielded them from the shells. On the top of the hill a battery[1] was arguing in tremendous roars with some other guns, and to the eye of the infantry, the artillerymen, the guns, the caissons,[2] the horses, were distinctly outlined upon the blue sky. When a piece was fired, a red streak as round as a log flashed low in the heavens, like a monstrous bolt of lightning. The men of the battery wore white duck trousers, which somehow emphasized their legs, and when they ran and crowded in little groups at the bidding of the shouting officers, it was more impressive than usual to the infantry.

Fred Collins of A Company was saying: "Thunder, I wisht I had a drink. Ain't there any water round here?" Then somebody yelled: "There goes th' bugler!"

[1] **battery:** set of heavy guns.

[2] **caissons:** ammunition wagons.

As the eyes of half of the regiment swept in one machine-like movement, there was an instant's picture of a horse in a great convulsive leap of a death wound and a rider leaning back with a crooked arm and spread fingers before his face. On the ground was the crimson terror of an exploding shell, with fibers of flame that seemed like lances. A glittering bugle swung clear of the rider's back as fell headlong the horse and the man. In the air was an odor as from a conflagration.[3]

Sometimes they of the infantry looked down at a fair little meadow which spread at their feet. Its long, green grass was rippling gently in a breeze. Beyond it was the gray form of a house half torn to pieces by shells and by the busy axes of soldiers who had pursued firewood. The line of an old fence was now dimly marked by long weeds and by an occasional post. A shell had blown the well house to fragments. Little lines of gray smoke ribboning upward from some embers indicated the place where had stood the barn.

From beyond a curtain of green woods there came the sound of some stupendous scuffle as if two animals of the size of islands were fighting. At a distance there were occasional appearances of swift-moving men, horses, batteries, flags, and, with the crashing of infantry, volleys were heard, often, wild and frenzied cheers. In the midst of it all, Smith and Ferguson, two privates of A Company, were engaged in a heated discussion, which involved the greatest questions of the national existence.

[3] **conflagration:** huge fire.

2. **REREAD** Reread lines 1–23. What is unexpected about Fred Collins's statement in lines 13–15? Support your answer with explicit textual evidence.

3. **READ** As you read lines 24–71, continue to cite textual evidence.

- Circle phrases that describe the meadow.
- In the margin, explain what happens to the house and barn in lines 24–31.
- Underline images in lines 40–50 that suggest fear and terror.

The battery on the hill presently engaged in a frightful duel. The white legs of the gunners scampered this way and that way and the officers redoubled their shouts. The guns, with their demeanors of **stolidity** and courage, were typical of something infinitely self-possessed in this clamor of death that swirled around the hill.

stolidity:

One of a "swing" team was suddenly smitten quivering to the ground and his maddened brethren dragged his torn body in their struggle to escape from this turmoil and danger. A young soldier astride one of the leaders swore and fumed in his saddle and furiously jerked at the bridle. An officer screamed out an order so violently that his voice broke and ended the sentence in a falsetto shriek.

The leading company of the infantry regiment was somewhat exposed and the colonel ordered it moved more fully under the shelter of the hill. There was the clank of steel against steel.

A lieutenant of the battery rode down and passed them, holding his right arm carefully in his left hand. And it was as if this arm was not at all a part of him, but belonged to another man. His sober and reflective charger went slowly. The officer's face was grimy and perspiring and his uniform was tousled as if he had been in direct grapple with an enemy. He smiled grimly when the men stared at him. He turned his horse toward the meadow.

Collins of A Company said: "I wisht I had a drink. I bet there's water in that there ol' well yonder!"

"Yes; but how you gain' to git it?"

For the little meadow which intervened was now suffering a terrible onslaught of shells. Its green and beautiful calm had vanished utterly. Brown earth was being flung in monstrous handfuls. And there was a massacre of the young blades of grass. They were being torn, burned, obliterated. Some curious fortune of the battle had made this gentle little meadow the object of the red hate of the shells and each one as it exploded seemed like an imprecation[4] in the face of a maiden.

[4] **imprecation:** curse.

4. **REREAD** Reread lines 64–71. How might the destruction of the meadow reflect the impact of war? Cite text evidence in your answer.

The wounded officer who was riding across this expanse said to himself: "Why, they couldn't shoot any harder if the whole army was massed here!"

A shell struck the gray ruins of the house and as, after the roar the shattered wall fell in fragments, there was a noise which resembled the flapping of shutters during a wild gale of winter. Indeed the infantry paused in the shelter of the bank, appeared as men standing upon a shore contemplating a madness of the sea. The angel of the calamity had under its glance the battery upon the hill. Fewer white-legged men labored about the guns. A shell had smitten one of the pieces and after the flare, the smoke, the dust, the wrath of this blow was gone, it was possible to see white legs stretched horizontally upon the ground. And at that interval to the rear, where it is the business of battery horses to stand with their noses to the fight awaiting the command to drag their guns out of the destruction or into it or wheresoever these incomprehensible humans demanded with whip and spur—in this line of passive and dumb spectators, whose fluttering hearts yet would not let them forget the iron laws of man's control of them—in this rank of brute soldiers there had been relentless and hideous carnage. From the ruck[5] of bleeding and **prostrate** horses, the men of the infantry could see one animal raising its stricken body with its forelegs and turning its nose with mystic and profound eloquence toward the sky.

prostrate:

Some comrades joked Collins about his thirst. "Well, if yeh want a drink so bad, why don't yeh go git it?"

"Well, I will in a minnet if yeh don't shut up."

A lieutenant of the artillery floundered his horse straight down the hill with as great concern as of it were level ground. As he

[5] **ruck:** mass, crowd.

5. READ ▶ As you read lines 72–94, circle the repeated image. In the margin, explain why Crane may have chosen to emphasize this image. Consider what the image may symbolize in your response.

galloped past the colonel of the infantry, he threw up his hand in a swift salute. "We've got to get out of that," he roared angrily. He was a black-bearded officer, and his eyes, which resembled beads, sparkled like those of an insane man. His jumping horse sped along the column of infantry.

The fat major standing carelessly with his sword held horizontally behind him and with his legs far apart, looked after the receding horseman and laughed. "He wants to get back with orders pretty quick or there'll be no batt'ry left," he observed.

The wise young captain of the second company hazarded to the lieutenant colonel that the enemy's infantry would probably soon attack the hill, and the lieutenant colonel snubbed him.

A private in one of the rear companies looked out over the meadow and then turned to a companion and said: "Look there, Jim." It was the wounded officer from the battery, who some time before had started to ride across the meadow, supporting his right arm carefully with his left hand. This man had encountered a shell apparently at a time when no one perceived him and he could now be seen lying face downward with a stirruped foot stretched across the body of his dead horse. A leg of the charger extended slantingly upward precisely as stiff as a stake. Around this motionless pair the shells still howled.

There was a quarrel in A Company. Collins was shaking his fist in the faces of some laughing comrades. "Dern yeh! I ain't afraid t' go. If yeh say much, I will go!"

"Of course, yeh will! Yeh'll run through that there medder, won't yeh?"

Collins said, in a terrible voice: "You see, now!" At this **ominous** threat his comrades broke into renewed jeers.

ominous:

6. READ ▶ As you read lines 95–154, continue to cite textual evidence.

- Underline what Collins says in response to his fellow officers.
- Circle the words the colonel uses to refer to Collins. In the margin, explain what this dialogue reveals about the colonel.

Collins gave them a dark scowl and went to find his captain. The latter was conversing with the colonel of the regiment.

"Captain," said Collins, saluting and standing at attention. In those days all trousers bagged at the knees. "Captain, I want t' git permission to go git some water from that there well over yonder!"

The colonel and the captain swung about simultaneously and stared across the meadow. The captain laughed. "You must be pretty thirsty, Collins?"

"Yes, sir; I am."

"Well—ah," said the captain. After a moment he asked: "Can't you wait?"

"No, sir."

The colonel was watching Collins's face. "Look here, my lad," he said, in a pious sort of a voice. "Look here, my lad." Collins was not a lad. "Don't you think that's taking pretty big risks for a little drink of water?"

"I dunno," said Collins, uncomfortably. Some of the resentment toward his companions, which perhaps had forced him into this affair, was beginning to fade. "I dunno wether 'tis."

The colonel and the captain contemplated him for a time.

"Well," said the captain finally.

"Well," said the colonel, "if you want to go, why, go."

Collins saluted. "Much obliged t' yeh."

As he moved away the colonel called after him. "Take some of the other boys' canteens with you an' hurry back now."

"Yes, sir. I will."

7. **◀ REREAD** Reread lines 95–154. What does Collins's dialogue reveal about his character? Support your answer with explicit text evidence.

8. **READ ▶** As you read lines 155–183, continue to cite text evidence.

- Underline details that describe Collins's appearance.
- In the margin, explain what is "curious" about Collins's manner.

> *I never thought Fred Collins had the blood in him for that kind of business.*

The colonel and the captain looked at each other then, for it had suddenly occurred that they could not for the life of them tell whether Collins wanted to go or whether he did not.

They turned to regard Collins and as they perceived him surrounded by **gesticulating** comrades the colonel said: "Well, by thunder! I guess he's going."

gesticulating:

Collins appeared as a man dreaming. In the midst of the questions, the advice, the warnings, all the excited talk of his company mates, he maintained a curious silence.

They were very busy in preparing him for his ordeal. When they inspected him carefully it was somewhat like the examination that grooms give a horse before a race; and they were amazed, staggered by the whole affair. Their astonishment found vent in strange repetitions.

"Are yeh sure a-goin'?" they demanded again and again.

"Certainly I am," cried Collins, at last furiously.

He strode sullenly away from them. He was swinging five or six canteens by their cords. It seemed that his cap would not remain firmly on his head, and often he reached and pulled it down over his brow.

There was a general movement in the compact column. The long animal-like thing moved slightly. Its four hundred eyes were turned upon the figure of Collins.

"Well, sir, if that ain't th' derndest thing. I never thought Fred Collins had the blood in him for that kind of business."

"What's he goin' to do, anyhow?"

"He's goin' to that well there after water."

"We ain't dyin' of thirst, are we? That's foolishness."

"Well, somebody put him up to it an' he's doin' it."

"Say, he must be a desperate cuss."

When Collins faced the meadow and walked away from the regiment, he was vaguely conscious that a chasm, the deep valley of all prides, was suddenly between him and his comrades. It was provisional, but the provision was that he return as a victor. He had blindly been led by quaint emotions and laid himself under an obligation to walk squarely up to the face of death.

But he was not sure that he wished to make a retraction even if he could do so without shame. As a matter of truth he was sure of very little. He was mainly surprised.

It seemed to him supernaturally strange that he had allowed his mind to maneuver his body into such a situation. He understood that it might be called dramatically great.

However, he had no full appreciation of anything excepting that he was actually conscious of being dazed. He could feel his dulled mind groping after the form and color of this incident.

Too, he wondered why he did not feel some keen agony of fear cutting his sense like a knife. He wondered at this because human expression had said loudly for centuries that men should feel afraid of certain things and that all men who did not feel this fear were phenomena—heroes.

9. REREAD Reread lines 164–183. What do you think finally provokes Collins's decision to leave the regiment and go to the well?

10. READ As you read lines 184–218, continue to cite textual evidence.

- Circle the phrases in 184–203 that describe Collins's thoughts and feelings about his situation.
- In the margin, explain why Collins thinks he is a hero.
- In lines 208–218, underline reasons why Collins says he is not a hero.

He was then a hero. He suffered that disappointment which we would all have if we discovered that we were ourselves capable of those deeds which we most admire in history and legend. This, then, was a hero. After all, heroes were not much.

No, it could not be true. He was not a hero. Heroes had no shames in their lives and, as for him, he remembered borrowing fifteen dollars from a friend and promising to pay it back the next day, and then avoiding that friend for ten months. When at home his mother had aroused him for the early labor of his life on the farm, it had often been his fashion to be irritable, childish, diabolical, and his mother had died since he had come to the war.

He saw that in this matter of the well, the canteens, the shells, he was an intruder in the land of fine deeds.

He was now about thirty paces from his comrades. The regiment had just turned its many faces toward him.

From the forest of terrific noises there suddenly emerged a little uneven line of men. They fired fiercely and rapidly at distant foliage on which appeared little puffs of white smoke. The spatter of skirmish firing was added to the thunder of the guns on the hill. The little line of men ran forward. A color sergeant fell flat with his flag as if he had slipped on ice. There was hoarse cheering from a distant field.

11. **REREAD** **Reread lines 184–218. What attributes does Collins possess that make him an unlikely hero? Cite explicit textual evidence in your response.**

12. **READ** **As you read lines 219–240, continue to cite text evidence.**

- **Underline images that appeal to your sense of hearing.**
- **In the margin, summarize what happens in lines 219–224.**
- **Circle details in lines 233–240 that describe the setting.**

CLOSE READ
Notes

Collins suddenly felt that two demon fingers were pressed into his ears. He could see nothing but flying arrows, flaming red. He lurched from the shock of this explosion, but he made a mad rush for the house, which he viewed as a man submerged to the neck in a boiling surf might view the shore. In the air, little pieces of shell howled and the earthquake explosions drove him insane with the menace of their roar. As he ran the canteens knocked together with a rhythmical tinkling.

As he neared the house, each detail of the scene became vivid to him. He was aware of some bricks of the vanished chimney lying on the sod. There was a door which hung by one hinge.

Rifle bullets called forth by the insistent skirmishers came from the far-off bank of foliage. They mingled with the shells and the pieces of shells until the air was torn in all directions by hootings, yells, howls. The sky was full of fiends who directed all their wild rage at his head.

13. **REREAD** Reread lines 219–240. How does Crane's word choice create a frightening mood? Support your answer with specific text evidence.

____

____

____

____

____

____

____

____

14. **READ** As you read lines 241–278, continue to cite text evidence.

- Underline phrases that provide details about the setting.
- In the margin, summarize what happens at the well.
- In the margin, write what the "long blue line of the regiment" may refer to.

"And now as he lay with his face turned away he was suddenly smitten with the terror."

When he came to the well he flung himself face downward and peered into its darkness. There were furtive silver glintings some feet from the surface. He grabbed one of the canteens and, unfastening its cap, swung it down by the cord. The water flowed slowly in with an **indolent** gurgle.

indolent:

And now as he lay with his face turned away he was suddenly smitten with the terror. It came upon his heart like the grasp of claws. All the power faded from his muscles. For an instant he was no more than a dead man.

The canteen filled with a maddening slowness in the manner of all bottles. Presently he recovered his strength and addressed a screaming oath to it. He leaned over until it seemed as if he intended to try to push water into it with his hands. His eyes as he gazed down into the well shone like two pieces of metal and in their expression was a great appeal and a great curse. The stupid water derided him.

There was the blaring thunder of a shell. Crimson light shone through the swift-boiling smoke and made a pink reflection on part of the wall of the well. Collins jerked out his arm and canteen with the same motion that a man would use in withdrawing his head from a furnace.

He scrambled erect and glared and hesitated. On the ground near him lay the old well bucket, with a length of rusty chain. He lowered it swiftly into the well. The bucket struck the water and then turning lazily over, sank. When, with hand reaching tremblingly over hand, he hauled it out, it knocked often against the walls of the well and spilled some of its contents.

In running with a filled bucket, a man can adopt but one kind of gait. So through this terrible field over which screamed practical angels of death Collins ran in the manner of a farmer chased out of a dairy by a bull.

His face went staring white with anticipation—anticipation of a blow that would whirl him around and down. He would fall as he had seen other men fall, the life knocked out of them so suddenly that their knees were no more quick to touch the ground than their heads. He saw the long blue line of the regiment, but his comrades were standing looking at him from the edge of an impossible star. He was aware of some deep wheel ruts and hoof prints in the sod beneath his feet.

The artillery officer who had fallen in this meadow had been making groans in the teeth of the tempest of sound. These futile cries, wrenched from him by his agony, were heard only by shells, bullets. When wild-eyed Collins came running, this officer raised himself. His face contorted and blanched from pain, he was about to utter some great beseeching cry. But suddenly his face straightened and he called: "Say, young man, give me a drink of water, will you?"

Collins had no room amid his emotions for surprise. He was mad from the threats of destruction.

"I can't," he screamed, and in this reply was a full description of his quaking apprehension. His cap was gone and his hair was riotous.

15. **REREAD** Reread lines 241–278. How does the author create a scary and chaotic mood in these lines? Support your answer with explicit textual evidence.

16. **READ** As you read lines 279–301, continue to cite textual evidence.

- Underline details that tell you the artillery officer is in pain.
- Circle details that describe Collins's physical appearence.
- In the margin, summarize Collins's actions in these lines.

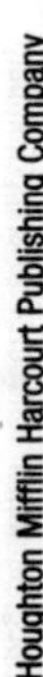

His clothes made it appear that he had been dragged over the ground by the heels. He ran on.

The officer's head sank down and one elbow crooked. His foot in its brass-bound stirrup still stretched over the body of his horse and the other leg was under the steed.

But Collins turned. He came dashing back. His face had now turned gray and in his eye was all terror. "Here it is! Here it is!"

The officer was as a man gone in drink. His arm bent like a twig. His head drooped as if his neck was of willow. He was sinking to the ground to lie face downward.

Collins grabbed him by the shoulder. "Here it is. Here's your drink. Turn over! Turn over, man, for God's sake!"

With Collins hauling at his shoulder, the officer twisted his body and fell with his face turned toward that region where lived the unspeakable noises of the swirling missiles. There was the faintest shadow of a smile on his lips as he looked at Collins. He gave a sigh, a little primitive breath like that from a child.

Collins tried to hold the bucket steadily, but his shaking hands caused the water to splash all over the face of the dying man. Then he jerked it away and ran on.

The regiment gave him a welcoming roar. The grimed faces were wrinkled in laughter.

His captain waved the bucket away. "Give it to the men!"

17. **◀ REREAD** Reread lines 279–301. Which details in these lines suggest that Collins acted heroically? Cite text evidence in your response.

____

____

____

____

18. **READ ▶** As you read lines 302–320, continue to cite textual evidence.

- Underline the officer's reaction to Collins's kindness.
- In the margin, restate what happens to the bucket of water.
- Circle the words used to describe the regiment.

The two genial, skylarking young lieutenants were the first to gain possession of it. They played over it in their fashion.

When one tried to drink, the other teasingly knocked his elbow. "Don't, Billie! You'll make me spill it," said the one. The other laughed.

Suddenly there was an oath, the thud of wood on the ground, and a swift murmur of astonishment from the ranks. The two lieutenants glared at each other. The bucket lay on the ground empty.

19. **REREAD AND DISCUSS** Reread lines 302–320. With a small group, discuss the story's ironic, or unexpected, ending. How does this ending affect your impression of the events in the story?

SHORT RESPONSE

Cite Text Evidence Explain whether you think Collins acted heroically during his mission to get the water. **Cite evidence** from the text and your reading notes to support your opinion.

Background Louisa May Alcott *(1832–1888) published her first work when she was 22, and she published over 30 books and story collections during her lifetime. In addition to writing literary masterworks such as* Little Women, *she is also known for the journal she kept during the Civil War. During the war she nursed wounded soldiers in Washington, D.C., hospitals. Army officials thought that female nurses would improve the morale of the wounded men, even though critics said the work was "indecent" for women and fretted that women would flirt with the soldiers. Alcott's journal proved critics wrong about female nurses.*

Civil War Journal

Journal Entries by Louisa May Alcott

1. READ ▶ As you read lines 1–21, begin to collect and cite text evidence.
   - In the margin, state when Alcott wrote the entry in lines 1–8.
   - Circle phrases that reveal Alcott's feelings about the war.
   - Underline reasons why Alcott wants to become a nurse.

1861

April.—War declared with the South, and our Concord company went to Washington. A busy time getting them ready, and a sad day seeing them off, for in a little town like this we all seem like one family in times like these. At the station the scene was very dramatic, as the brave boys went away perhaps never to come back again.

I've often longed to see a war, and now I have my wish. I long to be a man, but as I can't fight, I will **content** myself with working for those who can. . . .

content:

1862

September, October.— . . . War news bad. Anxious faces, beating hearts, and busy minds.

I like the stir in the air, and long for battle like a warhorse when he smells powder. The blood of the Mays is up![1] . . .

[1] **The blood of the Mays is up!:** The temper that Alcott has inherited from her ancestors (the Mays) is aroused.

CLOSE READ
Notes

November.—Thirty years old. Decided to go to Washington as a nurse if I could find a place. Help needed, and I love nursing, and *must* let out my pent-up energy in some new way. Winter is always a hard and a dull time, and if I am away there is one less to feed and warm and worry over.

I want new experiences, and am sure to get 'em if I go. So I've sent in my name, and bide my time[2] writing tales, to leave all snug behind me, and mending up my old clothes,—for nurses don't need nice things, thank goodness!

December.—On the 11th I received a note from Miss H. M. Stevenson telling me to start for Georgetown next day to fill a place in the Union Hotel Hospital. Mrs. Ropes of Boston was matron, and Miss Kendall of Plymouth was a nurse there, and though a hard place, help was needed. I was ready, and when my commander said "March!" I marched. Packed my trunk, and reported in B.[oston] that same evening.

We had all been full of courage till the last moment came, then we all broke down. I realized that I had taken my life in my hand, and might never see them all again. I said, "Shall I stay, Mother?" as I hugged her close. "No, go!" answered the Spartan[3] woman, and till I turned the corner she bravely smiled and waved her wet handkerchief on the doorstep. Shall I ever see that dear old face again?

---

[2] **bide my time:** wait around.

[3] **Spartan:** strong and self-disciplined.

2. REREAD Reread lines 1–21. How does Alcott use words with positive connotations to explain her desire to become a Civil War nurse? Support your answer with explicit textual evidence.

____

____

____

____

3. READ As you read lines 22–64, continue to cite textual evidence.

- Underline details in lines 22–37 that suggest a similarity between Alcott and a soldier.
- In the margin, paraphrase Alcott's thoughts in lines 48–49.
- Circle the little boy's description of Alcott in lines 52–64.

"I want new experiences, and am sure to get 'em if I go."

So I set forth in the December twilight, with May and Julian Hawthorne as escort, feeling as if I was the son of the house going to war.

Friday, the 12th, was a very memorable day, spent in running all over Boston to get my pass, etc., calling for parcels, getting a tooth filled, and buying a veil,—my only purchase. A. C. gave me some old clothes, the dear Sewalls money for myself and boys, lots of love and help, and at 5 P.M., saying "good-by" to a group of tearful faces at the station, I started on my long journey, full of hope and sorrow, courage and plans.

A most interesting journey into a new world full of stirring sights and sounds, new adventures, and an evergrowing sense of the great task I had undertaken.

I said my prayers as I went rushing through the country white with tents, all alive with patriotism, and already red with blood.

A solemn time, but I'm glad to live in it, and am sure it will do me good whether I come out alive or dead.

All went well, and I got to Georgetown one evening very tired. Was kindly welcomed, slept in my narrow bed with two other room-mates, and on the morrow began my new life by seeing a poor man die at dawn, and sitting all day between a boy with pneumonia and a man shot through the lungs. A strange day, but I did my best, and when I put mother's little black shawl round the boy while he sat up panting for breath, he smiled and said, "You are real motherly,

ma'am." I felt as if I was getting on. The man only lay and stared with his big black eyes, and made me very nervous. But all were well behaved, and I sat looking at the twenty strong faces as they looked back at me,—hoping that I looked "motherly" to them, for my thirty years made me feel old, and the suffering round me made me long to comfort every one. . . .

1863

January.—I never began the year in a stranger place than this, five hundred miles from home, alone among strangers, doing painful duties all day long, & leading a life of constant excitement in this greathouse surrounded by 3 or 4 hundred men in all stages of suffering, disease & death. Though often home sick, heart sick & worn out, I like it—find real pleasure in comforting tending & cheering these poor souls who seem to love me, to feel my sympathy though unspoken, & acknowledge my hearty good will in spite of the ignorance, awkwardness, & bashfulness which I cannot help showing in so new & trying a situation. The men are docile, respectful, & affectionate, with but few exceptions, truly lovable & manly many of them. John Suhre a Virginia blacksmith is the prince of patients, & though what we call a common man, in education & condition, to me is all that I could expect or ask from the first gentleman in the land. Under his plain speech & unpolished manner I seem to see a noble character, a heart as warm & tender as a woman's, a nature fresh &

4. **REREAD** **Reread lines 52–64. Alcott says she hopes to appear "motherly" to all her patients. How would your perception of Alcott change if she had used a word such as *watchful* or *protective,* which has a similar denotation but different connotation?**

5. **READ** **As you read lines 65–86, continue to cite text evidence.**

- **Underline details that describe Alcott's duties.**
- **Circle details that describe Alcott's patients, including John Suhre.**
- **In the margin, summarize Alcott's feelings about her experiences.**

frank as any child's. He is about thirty, I think, tall & handsome, mortally wounded & dying royally, without **reproach**, repining,[4] or remorse. Mrs. Ropes & myself love him & feel indignant that such a man should be so early lost, for though he might never distinguish himself before the world, his influence & example cannot be without effect, for real goodness is never wasted.

reproach:

Mon 4th—I shall record the events of a day as a sample of the days I spend—

Up at six, dress by gas light, run through my ward & fling up the windows though the men grumble & shiver; but the air is bad enough to breed a pestilence & as no notice is taken of our frequent appeals for better ventilation I must do what I can. Poke up the fire, add blankets, joke, coax & command, but continue to open doors & windows as if life depended on it; mine does, & doubtless many another, for a more perfect pestilence-box than this house I never saw—cold, damp, dirty, full of vile odors from wounds, kitchens, wash rooms, & stables. No competent head, male or female, to right matters, & a jumble of good, bad, & indifferent nurses, surgeons & attendants to complicate the Chaos still more.

After this unwelcome progress through my **stifling** ward I go to breakfast with what appetite I may; find the inevitable fried beef, salt butter, husky bread & washy coffee; listen to the clack of eight women & a dozen men; the first silly, stupid or possessed of but one idea, the last absorbed in their breakfast & themselves to a degree that is both **ludicrous** and provoking, for all the dishes are ordered down the table *full* & returned *empty*, the conversation is entirely among themselves

stifling:

ludicrous:

[4] **repining:** fretting, being discontented.

6. **REREAD AND DISCUSS** Reread lines 65–86. In a small group, compare and contrast Alcott's feelings about the war in this entry with the way she felt in previous journal entries. Cite explicit textual evidence in your discussion.

7. **READ** As you read lines 87–117, continue to cite textual evidence.
   - In the margin, restate what Alcott says about the journal entry for Monday the 4th in lines 87–88.
   - Circle the phrases that describe the conditions in the hospital.
   - Underline the description of Alcott's duties as a nurse on a typical day.

& each announces his opinion with an air of importance that frequently causes me to choke in my cup or bolt my meals with undignified speed lest a laugh betray to these pompous beings that a "child's among them takin' notes." Till noon I trot, trot, giving out rations, cutting up food for helpless "boys," washing faces, teaching my attendants how beds are made or floors swept, dressing wounds, taking Dr. FitzPatrick's orders, (privately wishing all the time that he would be more gentle with my big babies), dusting tables, sewing bandages, keeping my tray tidy, rushing up & down after pillows, bed linen, sponges, book & directions, till it seems as if I would joyfully pay down all I possess for a fifteen minutes rest.

8. **REREAD** Reread lines 87–117. Which details in these lines develop Alcott's concept of the poor working conditions in the hospital? Explain, citing explicit textual evidence in your answer.

SHORT RESPONSE

Cite Text Evidence Compare and contrast Alcott's journal entry in lines 1–64 with her entry in lines 87–117. Which concepts do each of these entries develop? Be sure to **cite text evidence** in your response.

COLLECTION 4

Approaching Adulthood

COLLECTION **4**

Approaching Adulthood

"When you become a teenager, you step onto a bridge. . . . The opposite shore is adulthood."

—Gail Carson Levine

SHORT STORY
The Whistle
Anne Estevis

Poems About Growing Up

POEM
Identity
Julio Noboa Polanco

POEM
Hard on the Gas
Janet S. Wong

NONFICTION
Much Too Young to Work So Hard
Naoki Tanaka

Background *An award-winning author,* **Anne Estevis** *(born 1936) grew up in Corpus Christi, Texas. Shortly after high school, she and her mother moved to a ranch in New Mexico. Her mother, a native New Mexican, was the family historian and storyteller. Through her stories, she imbued in her daughter an appreciation for the history and diverse cultures of Mexico and the American Southwest, which Estevis later used in her novels.*

The Whistle

Short Story by Anne Estevis

1. READ ▶ As you read lines 1–12, begin to cite text evidence.
   - Circle the reason the grandmother comes to live with the family.
   - Underline what the mother tells the abuela.
   - Underline what the mother tells her children.

My **paternal** grandmother Carmen was a tiny woman, not even five feet tall. She came to live with us because she said she needed to help my mother with the heavy load of raising a family. Having my grandmother around was usually pleasant; however, I remember a time when I wished she would find another family to care for. It was during the late autumn when I was fourteen years old. My parents had gone to San Antonio because my mother's father was very ill.

Before leaving, Mamá said to my abuela,[1] "Please take care of Chatita and the boys while I am gone."

Then Mamá turned around and quietly said to my brothers and me, "Children, please take care of your grandmother."

paternal:

[1] **abuela** (ä bwe' lə): Spanish for "Grandmother."

CLOSE READ
Notes

For several days we all took good care of one another. Then, on Saturday, the third day of my parents' absence, a cool front blew in a short while after we had eaten our noon meal. It wasn't terribly cold, just a little nippy.

My grandmother took note of the pleasant weather and remarked, "What a nice day it is! I think I will clean the storage shed." She retied her sagging apron, put on her sweater, and marched directly out to the shed.

While my grandmother toiled in the shed, I went about my Saturday chores as usual: washing the bedding, cleaning out the ice box, feeding the chickens, cleaning the lantern chimneys, and polishing my only pair of shoes. My brothers Keno and Chuy had been instructed by our father to prepare the fields for winter vegetable planting, so I was alone in the house. I liked it this way because I could do my work without interruption and get finished sooner.

In the late afternoon I took some vegetable peelings out to the chickens and noticed that the sky was cloudy and the wind was blowing harder than it had earlier. The day was turning cold. I glanced toward the storage shed and wondered how much longer my abuela would be working. I faintly heard what sounded like a goat bleating, so I looked around. Seeing nothing, I hurried back into the house to finish my chores. I especially wanted to get the lanterns put back together before dark.

2. **◀ REREAD** Reread lines 9–12. Write what you can infer about the mother's motivation for telling the children and the grandmother to take care of one another.

____

____

____

____

3. **READ ▶** As you read lines 13–48, continue to cite text evidence.

- Circle what the grandmother decides to do when the cool front arrives.
- Underline each of the narrator's chores.
- Explain in the margin how the weather changes and what the narrator hears as she finishes her chores.

Later I went out to get some firewood and while picking up small pieces of kindling from near the woodpile I heard again what I thought was a bleating goat. Still, I couldn't see the animal. Perhaps Keno or Chuy had brought home a kid to slaughter. They did that occasionally. We all enjoyed the **savory** meat of *cabrito*;[2] I was beginning to feel hungry just thinking about it. I thought I should look for the animal, but decided to get the fire in the stove going first because I could see Chuy coming toward the house on the tractor. Keno was already at the tractor shed, and the boys usually wanted coffee as soon as they got to the house.

savory:

The house quickly warmed from the fire in the cookstove. I was just putting on the pot for coffee when my brothers stomped into the kitchen.

"It's really getting cold out there!" said Chuy as he hovered over the big stove.

"Is the coffee ready, Chatita?" Keno asked.

I shook my head. "What about the goat? Are you going to butcher it?"

[2] **cabrito** (kä brē' tô): Spanish for the "meat of a young goat, or kid."

4. **REREAD** Reread lines 21–48. Briefly summarize what the characters are doing that day.

5. **READ** As you read lines 49–71, continue to cite text evidence.

- Underline what Chuy says about the weather and the goats.
- Explain in the margin what the narrator suddenly realizes when she hears Chuy's comment about the goats.

Neither answered. Chuy stopped warming his hands and turned away from the stove to look at me. Keno continued washing up in the enamel wash pan.

"I said, are you going to butcher the goat?"

"What goat are you talking about?" responded Keno.

"We don't have any goats," said Chuy.

I gasped and said, "Oh, my goodness! Come with me! Hurry!" I bounded out the kitchen door with my brothers behind me.

As we approached the storage shed I could see that the outside latch hook on the door was in place. I flipped the hook up and flung open the door. There, sitting on the floor, wrapped up in burlap bags like a mummy, was a cold and shivering grandmother. She tried to talk, but her voice was almost gone.

My brother helped the tiny woman to her feet and Keno carried her into the house as quickly as he could. All the way she was croaking like a frog, but I'm sure I discerned the words *"¡Huercos desgraciados!"* repeated over and over. This meant that we were wretched brats, or maybe worse.

6. **◀ REREAD** Reread lines 62–66 and continue to cite text evidence. What can you infer from knowing that the shed's latch hook was in place when the children found their grandmother? What can you infer about the bleating goat?

7. **READ ▶** As you read lines 72–93, continue to collect text evidence.
   - Underline what the narrator learns in lines 88–93.
   - In the margin, explain what the narrator could have done to keep her grandmother from being trapped.

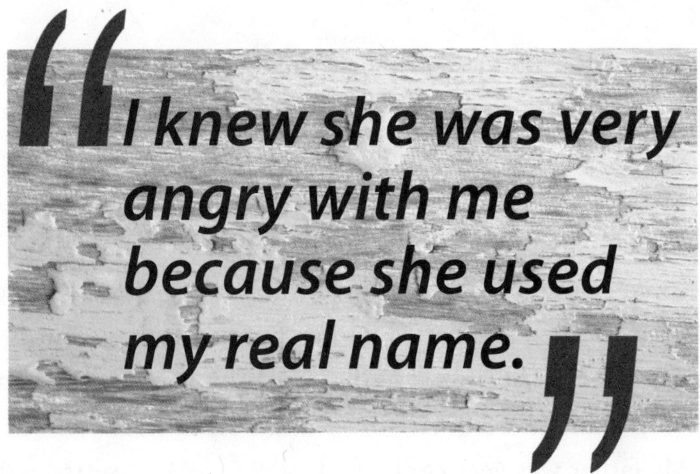

My brothers placed her in the chair nearest the kitchen stove while I fetched a soft woolen blanket to wrap her in. Chuy poured a cup of coffee and set it before her. Then we all sat down around the table staring at our obviously **infuriated** grandmother.

infuriated:

"What unfortunate children you are. You have no brains!" she said in a raspy voice. Her entire body was shivering. "You left me to die out there!" She shook her fist at each one of us and then looked squarely at me. "You, Telésfora. You must be deaf!" She shook a crooked index finger at me.

I knew she was very angry with me because she used my real name.

"I called and called for you. The wind blew the door shut and it locked. All afternoon I yelled, but you didn't come. I nearly froze to death!" She scowled and slowly turned her head away from me.

"But I didn't hear you," I answered. "I'm sorry. Please, Abuelita. I'm truly sorry!"

How could I have confused my grandmother's voice with that of a bleating goat? I felt terribly guilty and ashamed. I knew that the shed door was prone to latch by itself if it was slammed. That's why a wooden stake for propping the door open was usually kept nearby. But this time the stake had not been used, and now my grandmother was shaking and shivering and glaring at me.

8. **REREAD AND DISCUSS** With a small group, discuss whether the evidence in the text justifies the grandmother's feelings toward the narrator once she is rescued, and the narrator's feelings once she realizes the mistake she has made (lines 76–93).

"Just you wait, Telésfora. Just you wait until your father gets home. I'll have him punish you," she said and her bottom lip quivered and her nostrils flared.

My parents came home in a few days and of course the first thing that occurred was that Abuelita told her story to my father.

"Son, Telésfora left me locked in the storage shed all afternoon on Saturday. I called and called for her, but she declares she didn't hear me. She says she heard a goat bleating. Can you imagine that I could possibly sound like a goat?" my grandmother said.

My father was very concerned, of course. I admitted to him that, indeed, I had mistakenly thought I heard a goat and that I was terribly sorry that I hadn't checked on Abuelita as I should have. He scolded me severely. But this wasn't enough punishment, according to my grandmother, so she decided to penalize me herself by refusing to speak to me. This made me very sad, and it seemed to affect all of us. A sense of sorrow and discomfort permeated our family.

9. **READ ▶** As you read lines 94–109, continue to cite text evidence.

- Underline text evidence that confirms that the relationship between the narrator and her grandmother has taken a turn for the worse.
- In the margin, make an inference about Abuelita's motivation for "telling on" the narrator. What does this tell you about her?

10. **◀ REREAD** Reread lines 103–109, noting what the narrator tells her father in her own defense. What does this tell you about her personality?

> **"*. . . this wasn't enough punishment, according to my grandmother . . .*"**

Two weeks later I asked to go with my father to the big yellow store in town. While Papa made his purchases, I bought a silver whistle and a long piece of blue satin ribbon. I threaded the ribbon through the ring on the whistle and tied the ends of the ribbon together.

That evening, I placed the whistle in a little box and wrapped it in some colored paper. After supper, I approached my grandmother.

"This is for you, Abuelita. I'm terribly sorry about what happened to you in the shed. I hope you can forgive me."

My grandmother looked at me and said nothing. Then she took the box and opened it. She pulled the whistle out by its ribbon.

"Well, Telésfora, whatever is this for?" she asked, keeping her eyes on the whistle.

"It's to wear around your neck when you are outside. If you need me, just blow the whistle and I'll come to you," I said.

"And how can I be sure you'll hear this little whistle? You couldn't even hear me yelling at you!" But Abuela put it around her neck anyway.

"The next evening, while I was feeding the chickens, I heard a faint whistle. I stopped what I was doing and stood very still. Then I heard the whistle more distinctly. Yes! It was definitely coming from inside the storage shed. I rushed to the shed and found the door latched. That surprised me because the wind wasn't blowing at all.

11. **READ ▶** As you read lines 110–141, continue to cite textual evidence.

- Circle each use of the word *whistle.*
- In the margin, explain what idea the narrator might be emphasizing by repeating this word.
- Underline details of Abuelita's behavior in lines 128–141.

There was no way that the door could have slammed shut by itself. Something seemed really strange about this, and I was suspicious. I unlatched the door and opened it. There stood my grandmother with the whistle in her mouth. She quickly removed it and said, "I think your papá needs to do something about that crazy door latch. Don't you think so, Chatita?"

She hurried out of the shed and we started toward the house. I could see that she was smiling, and I think I even heard her chuckling.

12. REREAD Reread lines 128–141. How did Abuelita get locked in the shed this time? Cite text evidence in your response.

SHORT RESPONSE

Cite Text Evidence Explain what the whistle symbolizes for both Chatita and Abuelita. **Cite text evidence** to support your ideas.

Background *The Italian poet Salvatore Quasimodo once wrote that "Poetry is the revelation of a feeling that the poet believes to be interior and personal which the reader recognizes as his own." While you read the following poems, think about how each speaker feels about growing up. Perhaps you will relate to the feelings the poems express about approaching adulthood.*

Poems About Growing Up

Julio Noboa Polanco *(born 1949) grew up in the Bronx, a part of New York City. He now lives in Texas. Polanco wrote "Identity," his best-known poem, when he was in the eighth grade. He had just broken up with his girlfriend, an event that marked a turning point in the young poet's life. He continued to write poetry for many years until he decided to focus on writing essays and articles on educational and cultural issues.*

Janet S. Wong *(born 1962) decided to become a poet after working as a lawyer for several years. Many of Wong's poems are about her experiences as an Asian American. Wong has said that a poem is a bit like shouting—since it's impossible to yell for very long, "you have to decide what you really need to say, and say it quickly."*

1. READ ▷ As you read, collect and cite textual evidence.
   - Circle where flowers and weeds grow.
   - Underline what the speaker wants each time he says "I'd rather."
   - In the margin next to stanzas 2, 5, and 6, write one or two words that describe the speaker.

Identity

Julio Noboa Polanco

Let them be as flowers,
always watered, fed, guarded, admired,
but harnessed to a pot of dirt.

I'd rather be a tall, ugly weed,
clinging on cliffs, like an eagle
wind-wavering above high, jagged rocks.

To have broken through the surface of stone
to live, to feel exposed to madness
of the vast, eternal sky.

To be swayed by the breezes of an ancient sea,
carrying my soul, my seed, beyond the mountains of time
or into the abyss of the bizarre.

I'd rather be unseen, and if
then shunned by everyone
than to be a pleasant-smelling flower,
growing in clusters in the fertile valley
where they're praised, handled, and plucked
by greedy, human hands.

I'd rather smell of musty, green stench
than of sweet, fragrant lilac.
If I could stand alone, strong and free,
I'd rather be a tall, ugly weed.

2. REREAD Reread the poem. What can you infer about what the flowers and the weed represent?

SHORT RESPONSE

Cite Text Evidence Why does the speaker want to be a weed? Review your reading notes and be sure to **cite evidence from the text** in your response.

1. **READ ▶** As you read, collect and cite text evidence.

- Underline the two things the speaker compares in the first stanza.
- In the margin, explain what line 6 means.

Hard on the Gas
Janet S. Wong

My grandfather taught himself to drive
rough, the way he learned to live,

push the pedal, hard on the gas,
rush up to 50,
coast a bit,

rush, rest, rush, rest—

When you clutch the bar above your right shoulder
he shoots you a look that asks,
Who said the ride would be smooth?

2. **◀ REREAD AND DISCUSS** Reread the poem. With a small group, discuss why the grandfather "shoots a look" at the speaker. Why does the speaker clutch the bar? Cite evidence from the poem in your discussion.

SHORT RESPONSE

Cite Text Evidence This poem is about more than the grandfather's driving ability. Explain the message, or larger meaning, of the question "*Who said the ride would be smooth?*" **Cite text evidence** in your response.

Background *By the end of the nineteenth century, more than 1.5 million children under the age of fifteen were hard at work in the United States. By 1900, the number had increased to 2 million, and many people started to refer to child labor as "child slavery." Lewis Hine was a great crusader against child labor. A former schoolteacher, Hine's photographs for the National Child Labor Committee documented the dreadful working conditions inflicted on children as young as three years old. Two of Hine's photographs of children at work illustrate the article you are about to read.*

Much Too Young to Work So Hard

History Article by Naoki Tanaka

CLOSE READ Notes

1. **READ ▶** As you read lines 1–10, begin to collect text evidence.

- Circle the time and place cited at the beginning of the article.
- Underline the description of the boys' job.
- In the margin, explain what the author says about the working conditions in the first paragraph.

A Picture of Child Labor

The year is 1911. Boys, aged nine and ten, are working as coal breakers at a coal mine in Pennsylvania. They are sitting in rows on boards placed over conveyor belts that are carrying coal from the mine to large bins and dump trucks. The boys' job is to pick out any pieces of slate and stone embedded in the coal. The boys must watch very carefully because coal and slate look very much alike. A foreman, armed with a broom handle, raps the heads of boys who are not working hard or fast enough. The boys bend over the conveyor belts until their backs ache. Their faces are covered with soot. Often they have chronic coughs from breathing in air thick with coal dust.

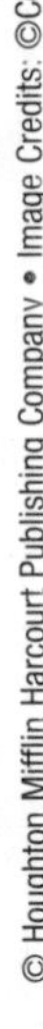

Breaker boys sorting coal, South Pittston, Pennsylvania, 1911; photograph by Lewis Hine. While Hine was taking photographs at a coal mine, two breaker boys fell into a coal chute and were smothered to death.

Small Hired Hands

Young girls were not exempt from such hard labor. During the early 1900s, when many crops were still planted and harvested by hand, children—both boys and girls—worked on farms in large numbers. People who were opposed to children working in factories often saw nothing wrong with them working on farms. After all, they were working with their families and breathing in fresh air. Some

2. REREAD Reread lines 1–10, and study the photograph on this page. What does the image add to your understanding of the boys' situation?

3. READ As you read lines 11–23, continue to cite text evidence.

- Circle each use of the words *girls, boys,* and *children.*
- Underline the positive opinion some people had about children working on farms. Then study the photograph of the children picking cotton. In the margin next to the image explain your reaction to that opinion.

This photograph, taken by Lewis Hine in 1913 at a farm in Bells, Texas, shows four children picking cotton.

children did help out on old-fashioned family farms. But many others traveled from farm to farm as hired hands doing the same backbreaking work as the adults. A 1913 photograph shows three girls and a boy, ranging in age from five to nine years, picking cotton in the sweltering Texas heat. Some of these cotton pickers were orphans. Others were the children of migrant workers. All of them picked cotton from dawn until the sun set.

Documenting Child Labor

In 1908, Lewis Hine wrote: "There is work that profits children, and there is work that brings profit only to employers. The object of

4. ◀ **REREAD AND DISCUSS** According to the Background information on page 83, many people in the 1900s thought that child labor was really "child slavery." With a small group, discuss whether the information presented in lines 11–23 and in the photograph on this page support this claim.

5. **READ** ▶ As you read lines 24–42, continue to cite text evidence.

- Paraphrase Hine's statement about the object of employing children in the margin.
- Underline Hine's purpose for exposing the hardships endured by working children.

employing children is not to train them, but to get high profits from their work." From 1908 until 1918, Hine documented in groundbreaking photographs children as young as three years old working long hours in often dangerous conditions. The children worked in factories, on farms, and in mines in the United States. As early as the 1830s, various states had passed laws restricting or prohibiting the employment of young children in industrial settings. Unfortunately, many of these laws were not enforced. Hine's goal was to publicize the fate of child laborers and the damage done to their young lives. His hope was that public outrage would stop the practice of employing children to do the work of adults.

America's army of child laborers had been growing steadily over the nineteenth century, fueled largely by an expanding economy. Factories, mines, and mills needed cheap labor, which children could and did supply. By 1911, more than 2 million American children under the age of sixteen were a regular part of the country's workforce.

Exploiting Children

Hine and others devoted to the rights of working children had no argument with children helping out with family tasks. Their focus was on the exploitation of children. Children were **exploited** because

exploited:

6. REREAD Reread lines 24–42. Summarize the information about "America's army of child laborers" (line 37).

7. READ As you read lines 43–81, continue to cite text evidence.

- Underline the reasons children were often exploited (lines 43–52).
- Underline the reasons cited by advocates for child labor (lines 53–60).
- In the margin, explain what finally stopped the practice of employing children.

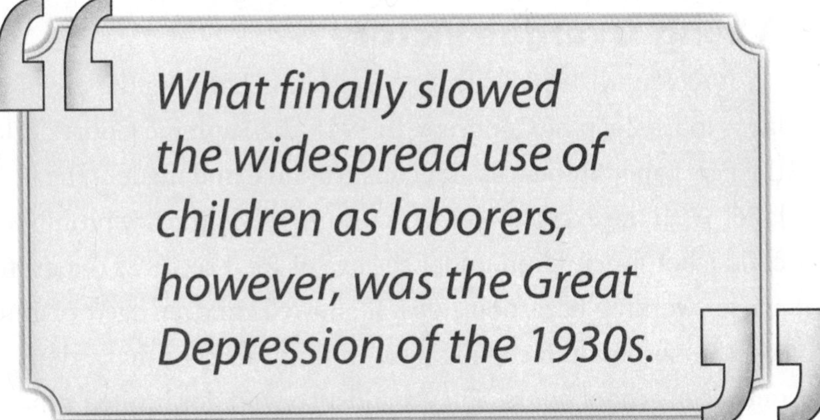

as workers their labor was cheap and because their age made them easy to order around. In addition, these working children were systematically robbed of education. Many were **illiterate,** and most had never attended school or, if they had, attended only sporadically. They were forced to be adults, shouldering adult responsibilities, long before they were ready. Finally, the work they did was dangerous and hazardous to their health.

illiterate:

Child-Labor Advocates

Those who argued for the continued use of children in industry and on farms argued that the work helped children develop a solid work ethic and that their work was necessary to support their impoverished families. Others claimed that after having worked hard labor, children would be more motivated to go back to school and become educated. Still others claimed that the cheap labor provided by children was needed to keep certain industries up and running, which in turn kept the nation's economy healthy.

The photographs of Louis Hine succeeded in publicizing and proving what many Americans had refused to believe: that numerous American children were being cruelly exploited. What finally slowed the widespread use of children as laborers, however, was the Great Depression of the 1930s. Sentiment against the use of child laborers had grown in the years preceding the Great Depression. With the economic catastrophe of the 1930s, however, many adults found themselves unemployed and struggling to find work. These adults wanted for themselves the jobs that traditionally had been held by children. Sadly, this more than any other reason may have turned the tide on using children as cheap labor in the United States.

A Long-Overdue Victory

It took until 1938 for federal legislation banning the use of child labor to finally pass Congress. In 1941, the Supreme Court declared the Fair Labor Standards Act constitutional and made it the law of the land. With the exception of agricultural work, the law prohibited child labor for children under the age of 16. It set 18 as the minimum age for working hazardous jobs. It allowed children aged 14 and 15 to work in non-manufacturing, non-mining, and non-hazardous jobs outside of school hours. They could also work for limited times during school vacations. In the fight to protect the rights of children, this law was a great and long-overdue victory.

8. **REREAD** Reread lines 72–81. Explain the way the passing of the Fair Labor Standards Act had an impact on the lives of children.

SHORT RESPONSE

Cite Text Evidence Using the text, the photographs, and your reading notes, explain why many people felt that child labor exploited children. **Cite text evidence** in your response.

COLLECTION 5

Anne Frank's Legacy

COLLECTION **5**

Anne Frank's Legacy

"I don't want to have lived in vain like most people . . . I want to go on living even after my death!"

—Anne Frank

DRAMA

The Diary of Anne Frank Act I, Scenes 1 and 2

Frances Goodrich and Albert Hackett

Background **Anne Frank** *was born in Germany in 1929. Her family relocated to the Netherlands in 1933 after the Nazi party came to power. In 1940, Germany invaded the Netherlands; in July 1942, the Frank and Van Daan families went into hiding. Anne's father survived the Holocaust. He was given Anne's diary at the end of World War II, and published it in 1947. It has since been translated into 67 languages and is considered one of the most affecting memoirs of the Holocaust.* **Frances Goodrich** *(1890–1984) and* **Albert Hackett** *(1900–1995) wrote the play called* The Diary of Anne Frank *based upon Anne's diary entries.*

The Diary of Anne Frank

Act I, Scenes 1 and 2

Drama by Frances Goodrich and Albert Hackett

CHARACTERS

SECRET ANNEX RESIDENTS

Anne Frank
Margot Frank
Mr. Frank
Mrs. Frank
Peter Van Daan
Mr. Van Daan
Mrs. Van Daan

WORKERS IN MR. FRANK'S BUSINESS

Miep Gies (mēp gēs)
Mr. Kraler (krä´lər)

A moveable bookcase hid the stairs to the hiding place, the Secret Annex.

1. READ ▷ As you read the stage directions and lines 1–42, begin to collect and cite text evidence.

- Underline details of the setting that show this is not an ordinary room.
- Circle the text that lets you know Mr. Frank has been through a very hard time.
- In the margin, make an inference about how Mr. Frank feels about being in the warehouse.

The Time. *July 1942–August 1944, November 1945*
The Place. *Amsterdam, the Netherlands*
The scene remains the same throughout the play. It is the top floor of a warehouse and office building in Amsterdam, Holland. The sharply peaked roof of the building is outlined against a sea of other rooftops, stretching away into the distance. Nearby is the belfry of a church tower, the Westertoren, whose carillon[1] *rings out the hours. Occasionally faint sounds float up from below: the voices of children playing in the street, the tramp of marching feet, a boat whistle from the canal.*

The three rooms of the top floor and a small attic space above are exposed to our view. The largest of the rooms is in the center, with two small rooms, slightly raised, on either side. On the right is a bathroom, out of sight. A narrow steep flight of stairs at the back leads up to the attic. The rooms are sparsely furnished with a few chairs, cots, a table or two. The windows are painted over, or covered with makeshift blackout curtains. In the main room there is a sink, a gas ring for cooking and a wood-burning stove for warmth.

The room on the left is hardly more than a closet. There is a skylight in the sloping ceiling. Directly under this room is a small steep stairwell, with steps leading down to a door. This is the only entrance from the building below. When the door is opened we see that it has been concealed on the outer side by a bookcase attached to it.

[1] **carillon:** a set of bells, commonly found in church bell towers.

ACT ONE

Scene 1

The curtain rises on an empty stage. It is late afternoon November, 1945.

The rooms are dusty, the curtains in rags. Chairs and tables are overturned.

The door at the foot of the small stairwell swings open. Mr. Frank *comes up the steps into view. He is a gentle, cultured European in his middle years. There is still a trace of a German accent in his speech.*

He stands looking slowly around, making a supreme effort at self-control. He is weak, ill.

His clothes are threadbare.

After a second he drops his rucksack on the couch and moves slowly about. He opens the door to one of the smaller rooms, and then abruptly closes it again, turning away. He goes to the window at the back, looking off at the Westertoren as its carillon strikes the hour of six, then he moves restlessly on.

From the street below we hear the sound of a barrel organ and children's voices at play. There is a many-colored scarf hanging from a nail. Mr. Frank *takes it, putting it around his neck. As he starts back for his rucksack, his eye is caught by something lying on the floor. It is a woman's white glove. He holds it in his hand and suddenly all of his self-control is gone. He breaks down, crying.*

We hear footsteps on the stairs. Miep Gies *comes up, looking for* Mr. Frank. Miep *is a Dutch girl of about twenty-two. She wears a coat and hat, ready to go home. She is pregnant. Her attitude toward* Mr. Frank *is protective, compassionate.*

Miep. Are you all right, Mr. Frank?

Mr. Frank (*quickly controlling himself*). Yes, Miep, yes.

Miep. Everyone in the office has gone home . . . It's after six. (*then pleading*) Don't stay up here, Mr. Frank. What's the use of torturing yourself like this?

Mr. Frank. I've come to say good-bye . . . I'm leaving here, Miep.

Miep. What do you mean? Where are you going? Where?

Mr. Frank. I don't know yet. I haven't decided.

Miep. Mr. Frank, you can't leave here! This is your home! Amsterdam is your home. Your business is here, waiting for you . . . You're needed here . . . Now that the war is over, there are things that . . .

Mr. Frank. I can't stay in Amsterdam, Miep. It has too many memories for me. Everywhere there's something . . . the house we lived in . . . the school . . . that street organ playing out there . . . I'm not the person you used to know, Miep. I'm a bitter old man. (*breaking off*) Forgive me. I shouldn't speak to you like this . . . after all that you did for us . . . the suffering . . .

Miep. No. No. It wasn't suffering. You can't say we suffered. (*As she speaks, she straightens a chair which is overturned.*)

Mr. Frank. I know what you went through, you and Mr. Kraler. I'll remember it as long as I live. (*He gives one last look around.*) Come, Miep.

(*He starts for the steps, then remembers his rucksack, going back to get it.*)

Miep (*hurrying up to a cupboard*). Mr. Frank, did you see? There are some of your papers here. (*She brings a bundle of papers to him.*) We found them in a heap of rubbish on the floor after . . . after you left.

Mr. Frank. Burn them.

(*He opens his rucksack to put the glove in it.*)

Miep. But, Mr. Frank, there are letters, notes . . .

Mr. Frank. Burn them. All of them.

Miep. Burn *this?*

(*She hands him a paperbound notebook.*)

Mr. Frank (*quietly*). Anne's diary. (*He opens the diary and begins to read.*) "Monday, the sixth of July, nineteen forty-two." (*to* Miep) Nineteen forty-two. Is it possible, Miep? . . . Only three years ago. (*As he continues his reading, he sits down on the couch.*) "Dear Diary, since you and I are going to be great friends, I will start by telling you about myself. My name is Anne Frank. I am thirteen years old. I was born in Germany the twelfth of June, nineteen twenty-nine. As my family is Jewish, we emigrated to Holland when Hitler came to power."

2. ◀ **REREAD AND DISCUSS** Reread lines 26–42. In a small group, discuss the clues that hint at what happened to Miep and Mr. Frank.

3. **READ** ▶ As you read lines 43–90, continue to cite textual evidence.

- Circle what Mr. Frank instructs Miep to do with the papers, and in the margin explain what this reveals about him.
- Underline what you learn about Anne from her diary.

(*As* Mr. Frank *reads on, another voice joins his, as if coming from the air. It is* Anne's Voice.)

Mr. Frank and Anne. "My father started a business, importing spice and herbs. Things went well for us until nineteen forty. Then the war came, and the Dutch **capitulation**, followed by the arrival of the Germans. Then things got very bad for the Jews."

capitulation:

(Mr. Frank's Voice *dies out.* Anne's Voice *continues alone. The lights dim slowly to darkness. The curtain falls on the scene.*)

Anne's Voice. You could not do this and you could not do that. They forced Father out of his business. We had to wear yellow stars.[2] I had to turn in my bike. I couldn't go to a Dutch school any more. I couldn't go to the movies, or ride in an automobile, or even on a streetcar, and a million other things. But somehow we children still managed to have fun. Yesterday Father told me we were going into hiding. Where, he wouldn't say. At five o'clock this morning Mother woke me and told me to hurry and get dressed. I was to put on as many clothes as I could. It would look too suspicious if we walked along carrying suitcases. It wasn't until we were on our way that I learned where we were going. Our hiding place was to be upstairs in the building where Father used to have his business. Three other people were coming in with us . . . the Van Daans and their son Peter . . . Father knew the Van Daans but we had never met them . . .

(*During the last lines the curtain rises on the scene. The lights dim on.* Anne's Voice *fades out.*)

[2] **yellow stars:** the six-pointed Stars of David that the Nazis ordered all Jews to wear for identification.

4. REREAD Reread lines 58–90. How does the structure of the drama change? What is the effect of this change?

Scene 2

It is early morning, July, 1942. The rooms are bare, as before, but they are now clean and orderly.

Mr. Van Daan, *a tall, portly man in his late forties, is in the main room, pacing up and down, nervously smoking a cigarette. His clothes and overcoat are expensive and well cut.*

Mrs. Van Daan *sits on the couch, clutching her possessions, a hatbox, bags, etc. She is a pretty woman in her early forties. She wears a fur coat over her other clothes.*

Peter Van Daan *is standing at the window of the room on the right, looking down at the street below. He is a shy, awkward boy of sixteen. He wears a cap, a raincoat, and long Dutch trousers, like "plus fours."*[3] *At his feet is a black case, a carrier for his cat.*

The yellow Star of David is conspicuous on all of their clothes.

Mrs. Van Daan (*rising, nervous, excited*). Something's happened to them! I know it!

Mr. Van Daan. Now, Kerli!

Mrs. Van Daan. Mr. Frank said they'd be here at seven o'clock. He said . . .

Mr. Van Daan. They have two miles to walk. You can't expect . . .

Mrs. Van Daan. They've been picked up. That's what's happened. They've been taken . . .

(Mr. Van Daan *indicates that he hears someone coming.*)

Mr. Van Daan. You see?

(Peter *takes up his carrier and his schoolbag, etc., and goes into the main room as* Mr. Frank *comes up the stairwell from below.* Mr. Frank *looks much younger now. His movements are brisk, his manner confident. He wears an overcoat and carries his hat and a small cardboard box. He crosses to the* Van Daans, *shaking hands with each of them.*)

---

[3] **plus fours:** pants that end just below the knee.

5. READ ▷ As you read lines 91–147, continue to cite text evidence.

- Circle the stage directions that explain the setting.
- Underline what the Van Daans are wearing, and write in the margin what this tells you about people who went into hiding.

Mr. Frank. Mrs. Van Daan, Mr. Van Daan, Peter. (*then, in explanation of their lateness*) There were too many of the Green Police[4] on the streets . . . we had to take the long way around.

(*Up the steps come* Margot Frank, Mrs. Frank, Miep [*not pregnant now*] *and* Mr. Kraler. *All of them carry bags, packages, and so forth. The Star of David is* **conspicuous** *on all of the* Franks' *clothing.* Margot *is eighteen, beautiful, quiet, shy.* Mrs. Frank *is a young mother, gently bred, reserved. She, like* Mr. Frank, *has a slight German accent.* Mr. Kraler *is a Dutchman, dependable, kindly.*

As Mr. Kraler *and* Miep *go upstage to put down their parcels,* Mrs. Frank *turns back to call* Anne.)

conspicuous:

Mrs. Frank. Anne?

(Anne *comes running up the stairs. She is thirteen, quick in her movements, interested in everything,* **mercurial** *in her emotions. She wears a cape, long wool socks and carries a schoolbag.*)

mercurial:

Mr. Frank (*introducing them*). My wife, Edith. Mr. and Mrs. Van Daan (Mrs. Frank *hurries over, shaking hands with them.*) . . . their son, Peter . . . my daughters, Margot and Anne.

(Anne *gives a polite little curtsy as she shakes* Mr. Van Daan's *hand. Then she immediately starts off on a tour of investigation of her new home, going upstairs to the attic room.* Miep *and* Mr. Kraler *are putting the various things they have brought on the shelves.*)

Mr. Kraler. I'm sorry there is still so much confusion.

Mr. Frank. Please. Don't think of it. After all, we'll have plenty of leisure to arrange everything ourselves.

Miep (*to* Mrs. Frank). We put the stores of food you sent in here. Your drugs are here . . . soap, linen here.

Mrs. Frank. Thank you, Miep.

[4] **Green Police:** the Nazi police who wore green uniforms.

6. **REREAD AND DISCUSS** Reread lines 142–147. In a small group, discuss why Miep and Mr. Kraler are helping the Franks and the Van Daans. How do you think Miep and Mr. Kraler feel about helping them?

Miep. I made up the beds . . . the way Mr. Frank and Mr. Kraler said. (*She starts out.*) Forgive me. I have to hurry. I've got to go to the other side of town to get some ration books[5] for you.

Mrs. Van Daan. Ration books? If they see our names on ration books, they'll know we're here.

Mr. Kraler. There isn't anything . . .
Miep. Don't worry. Your names won't be on them. (*as she hurries out*) I'll be up later.
} *Together*

Mr. Frank. Thank you, Miep.

Mrs. Frank (*to* Mr. Kraler). It's illegal, then, the ration books? We've never done anything illegal.

Mr. Frank. We won't be living here exactly according to regulations. (*As* Mr. Kraler *reassures* Mrs. Frank, *he takes various small things, such as matches, soap, etc., from his pockets, handing them to her.*)

Mr. Kraler. This isn't the black market,[6] Mrs. Frank. This is what we call the white market . . . helping all of the hundreds and hundreds who are hiding out in Amsterdam.

(*The carillon is heard playing the quarter-hour before eight.* Mr. Kraler *looks at his watch.* Anne *stops at the window as she comes down the stairs.*)

Anne. It's the Westertoren!

Mr. Kraler. I must go. I must be out of here and downstairs in the office before the workmen get here. (*He starts for the stairs leading*

[5] **ration books:** books of stamps or coupons issued by the government in wartime. With these coupons, people could purchase scarce items, such as food, clothing, and gasoline.

[6] **black market:** a system for selling goods illegally, in violation of rationing and other restrictions.

7. READ ▶ As you read lines 148–201, continue to cite evidence from the text.

- Underline examples of Mr. Kraler's words and actions toward the Franks and Van Daans. In the margin, explain what they reveal about his character.
- Circle the clothing that the Franks and Van Daans are wearing, and explain in the margin why they are wearing so many layers of clothing.

CLOSE READ Notes

out.) Miep or I, or both of us, will be up each day to bring you food and news and find out what your needs are. Tomorrow I'll get you a better bolt for the door at the foot of the stairs. It needs a bolt that you can throw yourself and open only at our signal. (*to* Mr. Frank) Oh . . . You'll tell them about the noise?

Mr. Frank. I'll tell them.

Mr. Kraler. Good-bye then for the moment. I'll come up again, after the workmen leave.

Mr. Frank. Good-bye, Mr. Kraler.

Mrs. Frank (*shaking his hand*). How can we thank you? (*The others murmur their good-byes.)*

Mr. Kraler. I never thought I'd live to see the day when a man like Mr. Frank would have to go into hiding. When you think—(*He breaks off, going out.* Mr. Frank *follows him down the steps, bolting the door after him. In the interval before he returns,* Peter *goes over to* Margot, *shaking hands with her. As* Mr. Frank *comes back up the steps,* Mrs. Frank *questions him anxiously.*)

Mrs. Frank. What did he mean, about the noise?

Mr. Frank. First let us take off some of these clothes. (*They all start to take off garment after garment. On each of their coats, sweaters, blouses, suits, dresses, is another yellow Star of David.* Mr. *and* Mrs. Frank *are underdressed quite simply. The others wear several things, sweaters, extra dresses, bathrobes, aprons, nightgowns, etc.*)

Mr. Van Daan. It's a wonder we weren't arrested, walking along the streets . . . Petronella with a fur coat in July . . . and that cat of Peter's crying all the way.

Anne (*as she is removing a pair of panties*). A cat?

Mrs. Frank (*shocked*). Anne, please!

Anne. It's all right. I've got on three more. (*She pulls off two more. Finally, as they have all removed their surplus clothes, they look to* Mr. Frank, *waiting for him to speak.*)

8. **REREAD** Reread lines 165–168. What do these lines reveal about Anne's character?

The view from a window in the Secret Annex.

Mr. Frank. Now. About the noise. While the men are in the building below, we must have complete quiet. Every sound can be heard down there, not only in the workrooms, but in the offices too. The men come at about eight-thirty, and leave at about five-thirty. So, to be perfectly safe, from eight in the morning until six in the evening we must move only when it is necessary, and then in stockinged feet. We must not speak above a whisper. We must not run any water. We cannot use the sink, or even, forgive me, the w.c.[7] The pipes go down through the workrooms. It would be heard. No trash . . . (Mr. Frank *stops* ***abruptly*** *as he hears the sound of marching feet from the street below. Everyone is motionless, paralyzed with fear.* Mr. Frank *goes quietly into the room on the right to look down out of the window.* Anne *runs after him, peering out with him. The tramping feet pass without stopping. The tension is relieved.* Mr. Frank, *followed by* Anne, *returns to the main room and resumes his instructions to the group.)* . . . No trash must ever be thrown out which might reveal that someone is living up here . . . not even a potato paring. We must burn everything in the stove at night. This is the way we must live until it is over, if we are to survive.

(*There is silence for a second.*)

abruptly:

[7] **w.c.:** water closet; toilet.

9. READ ▶ As you read lines 202–266, continue to cite evidence from the text.

- Underline the rules that the Franks and Van Daans must follow.
- Circle ways in which Mr. Frank makes the situation more normal.

Mrs. Frank. Until it is over.

Mr. Frank (*reassuringly*). After six we can move about . . . we can talk and laugh and have our supper and read and play games . . . just as we would at home. (*He looks at his watch.*) And now I think it would be wise if we all went to our rooms, and were settled before eight o'clock. Mrs. Van Daan, you and your husband will be upstairs. I regret that there's no place up there for Peter. But he will be here, near us. This will be our common room, where we'll meet to talk and eat and read, like one family.

Mr. Van Daan. And where do you and Mrs. Frank sleep?

Mr. Frank. This room is also our bedroom.

Mrs. Van Daan. That isn't right. We'll sleep here and you take the room upstairs.

Mr. Van Daan. It's your place.

} *Together*

Mr. Frank. Please. I've thought this out for weeks. It's the best arrangement. The only arrangement.

Mrs. Van Daan (*to* Mr. Frank). Never, never can we thank you. (*then to* Mrs. Frank) I don't know what would have happened to us, if it hadn't been for Mr. Frank.

Mr. Frank. You don't know how your husband helped me when I came to this country . . . knowing no one . . . not able to speak the language. I can never repay him for that. (*going to* Van Daan) May I help you with your things?

Mr. Van Daan. No. No. (*to* Mrs. Van Daan) Come along, *liefje*.[8]

Mrs. Van Daan. You'll be all right, Peter? You're not afraid?

Peter (*embarrassed*). Please, Mother.

(*They start up the stairs to the attic room above.* Mr. Frank *turns to* Mrs. Frank.)

Mr. Frank. You too must have some rest, Edith. You didn't close your eyes last night. Nor you, Margot.

Anne. I slept, Father. Wasn't that funny? I knew it was the last night in my own bed, and yet I slept soundly.

---

[8] **liefje** (lēf'yə): *Dutch*: little darling.

Mr. Frank. I'm glad, Anne. Now you'll be able to help me straighten things in here. (*to* Mrs. Frank *and* Margot) Come with me . . . You and Margot rest in this room for the time being. (*He picks up their clothes, starting for the room on the right.*)

Mrs. Frank. You're sure . . .? I could help . . . And Anne hasn't had her milk . . .

Mr. Frank. I'll give it to her. (*to* Anne *and* Peter) Anne, Peter . . . it's best that you take off your shoes now, before you forget. (*He leads the way to the room, followed by* Margot.)

Mrs. Frank. You're sure you're not tired, Anne?

Anne. I feel fine. I'm going to help Father.

Mrs. Frank. Peter, I'm glad you are to be with us.

Peter. Yes, Mrs. Frank.

(Mrs. Frank *goes to join* Mr. Frank *and* Margot.)

(*During the following scene* Mr. Frank *helps* Margot *and* Mrs. Frank *to hang up their clothes. Then he persuades them both to lie down and rest. The* Van Daans *in their room above settle themselves. In the main room* Anne *and* Peter *remove their shoes.* Peter *takes his cat out of the carrier.*)

Anne. What's your cat's name?

Peter. Mouschi.[9]

---

[9] **Mouschi** (mōō'shē).

10. REREAD Reread lines 222–262. Why is it important for Mr. Frank to normalize the situation? Support your answer with explicit textual evidence.

11. READ As you read lines 267–325, continue to cite evidence from the text.

- Underline the questions Anne asks Peter, and explain in the margin what is significant about their exchange.
- Circle stage directions that explain what Anne and Peter do to their Star of David badges.

Anne. Mouschi! Mouschi! Mouschi! (*She picks up the cat, walking away with it. To* Peter.) I love cats. I have one . . . a darling little cat. But they made me leave her behind. I left some food and a note for the neighbors to take care of her . . . I'm going to miss her terribly. What is yours? A him or a her?

Peter. He's a tom. He doesn't like strangers.

(*He takes the cat from her, putting it back in its carrier.*)

Anne (*unabashed*). Then I'll have to stop being a stranger, won't I? Is he fixed?

Peter (*startled*). Huh?

Anne. Did you have him fixed?

Peter. No.

Anne. Oh, you ought to have him fixed—to keep him from—you know, fighting. Where did you go to school?

Peter. Jewish Secondary.

Anne. But that's where Margot and I go! I never saw you around.

Peter. I used to see you . . . sometimes . . .

Anne. You did?

Peter. . . . in the school yard. You were always in the middle of a bunch of kids. (*He takes a penknife from his pocket.*)

Anne. Why didn't you ever come over?

Peter. I'm sort of a lone wolf. (*He starts to rip off his Star of David.*)

Anne. What are you doing?

Peter. Taking it off.

Anne. But you can't do that. They'll arrest you if you go out without your star.

(*He tosses his knife on the table.*)

Peter. Who's going out?

Anne. Why, of course! You're right! Of course we don't need them any more. (*She picks up his knife and starts to take her star off.*) I wonder what our friends will think when we don't show up today?

Peter. I didn't have any dates with anyone.

Anne. Oh, I did. I had a date with Jopie to go and play ping-pong at her house. Do you know Jopie de Waal?[10]

Peter. No.

Anne. Jopie's my best friend. I wonder what she'll think when she telephones and there's no answer? . . . Probably she'll go over to the house . . . I wonder what she'll think . . . we left everything as if we'd suddenly been called away . . . breakfast dishes in the sink . . . beds not made . . . (*As she pulls off her star, the cloth underneath shows clearly the color and form of the star.*) Look! It's still there! (Peter *goes over to the stove with his star.*) What're you going to do with yours?

Peter. Burn it.

Anne (*She starts to throw hers in, and cannot.*) It's funny, I can't throw mine away. I don't know why.

Peter. You can't throw . . .? Something they branded you with . . .? That they made you wear so they could spit on you?

Anne. I know. I know. But after all, it *is* the Star of David, isn't it?

(*In the bedroom, right,* Margot *and* Mrs. Frank *are lying down.* Mr. Frank *starts quietly out.*)

Peter. Maybe it's different for a girl.

(Mr. Frank *comes into the main room.*)

Mr. Frank. Forgive me, Peter. Now let me see. We must find a bed for your cat. (*He goes to a cupboard.*) I'm glad you brought your cat. Anne was feeling so badly about hers. (*getting a used small washtub*) Here we are. Will it be comfortable in that?

---

[10] **Jopie de Waal** (yō'pē də väl').

12. REREAD Reread lines 291–325. What do Peter's words and actions reveal about his character?

13. READ As you read lines 326–388, continue to cite text evidence.

- Underline several examples of dialogue that reveal different aspects of Mr. Frank's personality, and describe his behavior in the margin.
- Explain in the margin how the diary helps you understand Scene 1.
- Circle the advice Mr. Frank tells Anne to remember and write in the margin why this advice is important.

“I’m going to think of it as a boarding house. A very peculiar summer boarding house . . .”

Peter (*gathering up his things*). Thanks.

Mr. Frank (*opening the door of the room on the left*). And here is your room. But I warn you, Peter, you can’t grow any more. Not an inch, or you’ll have to sleep with your feet out of the skylight. Are you hungry?

Peter. No.

Mr. Frank. We have some bread and butter.

Peter. No, thank you.

Mr. Frank. You can have it for luncheon then. And tonight we will have a real supper . . . our first supper together.

Peter. Thanks. Thanks.

(*He goes into his room. During the following scene he arranges his possessions in his new room.*)

Mr. Frank. That’s a nice boy, Peter.

Anne. He’s awfully shy, isn’t he?

Mr. Frank. You’ll like him, I know.

Anne. I certainly hope so, since he’s the only boy I’m likely to see for months and months.

(Mr. Frank *sits down, taking off his shoes.*)

Mr. Frank. Annele,[11] there’s a box there. Will you open it?

(*He indicates a carton on the couch. Anne brings it to the center table. In the street below there is the sound of children playing.*)

Anne (*as she opens the carton*). You know the way I’m going to think of it here? I’m going to think of it as a boarding house. A very peculiar summer boarding house, like the one that we—(*She breaks off as she pulls out some photographs.*) Father! My movie stars! I was wondering

[11] **Annele/Anneke:** a nickname for Anne.

where they were! I was looking for them this morning . . . and Queen Wilhelmina! How wonderful!

Mr. Frank. There's something more. Go on. Look further.

(*He goes over to the sink, pouring a glass of milk from a thermos bottle.*)

Anne (*pulling out a pasteboard-bound book*). A diary! (*She throws her arms around her father.*) I've never had a diary. And I've always longed for one. (*She looks around the room.*) Pencil, pencil, pencil, pencil. (*She starts down the stairs.*) I'm going down to the office to get a pencil.

Mr. Frank. Anne! No! (*He goes after her, catching her by the arm and pulling her back.*)

Anne (*startled*). But there's no one in the building now.

Mr. Frank. It doesn't matter. I don't want you ever to go beyond that door.

Anne (*sobered*). Never . . .? Not even at nighttime, when everyone is gone? Or on Sundays? Can't I go down to listen to the radio?

Mr. Frank. Never. I am sorry, Anneke. It isn't safe. No, you must never go beyond that door.

(*For the first time* Anne *realizes what "going into hiding" means.*)

Anne. I see.

Mr. Frank. It'll be hard, I know. But always remember this, Anneke. There are no walls, there are no bolts, no locks that anyone can put on your mind. Miep will bring us books. We will read history, poetry, mythology. (*He gives her the glass of milk.*) Here's your milk. (*With his arm about her, they go over to the couch, sitting down side by side.*) As a matter of fact, between us, Anne, being here has certain advantages for you. For instance, you remember the battle you had with your mother the other day on the subject of overshoes? You said you'd rather die than wear overshoes. But in the end you had to wear them? Well now, you see, for as long as we are here you will never have to wear overshoes! Isn't that good? And the coat that you inherited from Margot, you won't have to wear that any more. And the piano! You won't have to practice on the piano. I tell you, this is going to be a fine life for you!

14. **REREAD AND DISCUSS** Reread lines 360–377. Think about Mr. Frank's advice. In a small group, discuss why he might have given the diary to Anne.

(Anne's *panic is gone.* Peter *appears in the doorway of his room, with a saucer in his hand. He is carrying his cat.)*

Peter. I . . . I . . . I thought I'd better get some water for Mouschi before . . .

Mr. Frank. Of course.

(As he starts toward the sink the carillon begins to chime the hour of eight. He tiptoes to the window at the back and looks down at the street below. He turns to Peter, *indicating in pantomime that it is too late.* Peter *starts back for his room. He steps on a creaking board. The three of them are frozen for a minute in fear. As* Peter *starts away again,* Anne *tiptoes over to him and pours some of the milk from her glass into the saucer for the cat.* Peter *squats on the floor, putting the milk before the cat.* Mr. Frank *gives* Anne *his fountain pen, and then goes into the room at the right. For a second* Anne *watches the cat, then she goes over to the center table, and opens her diary.*

In the room at the right, Mrs. Frank *has sat up quickly at the sound of the carillon.* Mr. Frank *comes in and sits down beside her on the settee, his arm comfortingly around her.*

Upstairs, in the attic room, Mr. *and* Mrs. Van Daan *have hung their clothes in the closet and are now seated on the iron bed.* Mrs. Van Daan *leans back exhausted.* Mr. Van Daan *fans her with a newspaper.*

Anne *starts to write in her diary. The lights dim out, the curtain falls.*

In the darkness Anne's Voice *comes to us again, faintly at first, and then with growing strength.)*

Anne's Voice. I expect I should be describing what it feels like to go into hiding. But I really don't know yet myself. I only know it's funny never to be able to go outdoors . . . never to breathe fresh air . . . never to run and shout and jump. It's the silence in the nights that frightens me most. Every time I hear a creak in the house, or a step on the street outside, I'm sure they're coming for us. The days aren't so bad. At least we know that Miep and Mr. Kraler are down there below us

15. **READ ▶** As you read lines 389–430, continue to cite text evidence.

- Explain in the margin what Anne's actions as described in the stage directions reveal about her character, and underline examples to support your conclusion.
- Circle what Anne says it means to be in hiding.

in the office. Our protectors, we call them. I asked Father what would happen to them if the Nazis found out they were hiding us. Pim said that they would suffer the same fate that we would . . . Imagine! They know this, and yet when they come up here, they're always cheerful and gay as if there were nothing in the world to bother them . . . Friday, the twenty-first of August, nineteen forty-two. Today I'm going to tell you our general news. Mother is unbearable. She insists on treating me like a baby, which I loathe. Otherwise things are going better. The weather is . . .

(*As* Anne's Voice *is fading out, the curtain rises on the scene.*)

16. REREAD Reread lines 414–429. Anne's reading from her diary is a form of soliloquy, a speech in which a character speaks private thoughts aloud. What is the effect of Anne's reading from her diary?

SHORT RESPONSE

Cite Text Evidence When does Anne begin to understand what going into hiding will mean? Describe some of the ways life in the secret annex is different from life outside. Review your reading notes, and be sure to **cite text evidence** in your response.

COLLECTION 6

The Value of Work

COLLECTION 6

The Value of Work

"Every job is a learning experience, and we can develop and grow in every one."

—Colin Powell

Background **Ray Bradbury** *wrote hundreds of short stories in his 70-year career. He has said he tells tales to warn people about the dangers in the world around them. You are about to read a story that takes place in the distant past. As you read, think about the way this story connects to the world today. Then, read the graphic version of "The Flying Machine," illustrated by* **Bernard Krigstein.**

COMPARING VERSIONS OF

The Flying Machine

CLOSE READ Notes

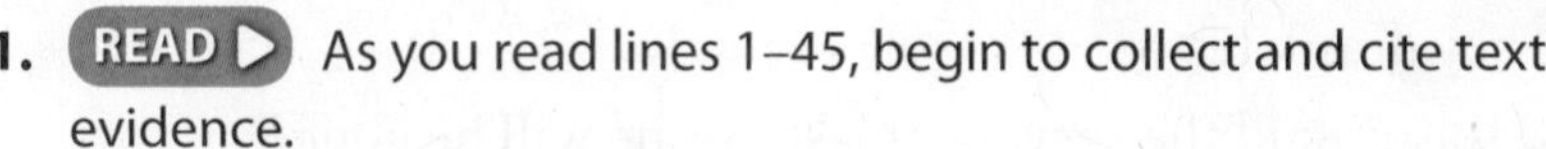

1. READ ▷ As you read lines 1–45, begin to collect and cite text evidence.
   - Circle repetitions of the word *miracle*. In the margin, state what the emperor says are miracles.
   - Circle what the servant says he sees.
   - Underline imagery that describes what they see.

The Flying Machine

Short Story by Ray Bradbury

In the year A.D. 400, the Emperor Yuan held his throne by the Great Wall of China, and the land was green with rain, readying itself toward the harvest, at peace, the people in his dominion[1] neither too happy nor too sad.

Early on the morning of the first day of the first week of the second month of the new year, the Emperor Yuan was sipping tea and fanning himself against a warm breeze when a servant ran across the scarlet and blue garden tiles, calling, "Oh, Emperor, Emperor, a miracle!"

"Yes" said the Emperor, "the air *is* sweet this morning."

"No, no, a miracle!" said the servant, bowing quickly.

"And this tea is good in my mouth, surely that is a miracle."

[1] **dominion:** country; territory.

"No, no, Your Excellency."

"Let me guess then—the sun has risen and a new day is upon us. Or the sea is blue. *That* now is the finest of all miracles."

"Excellency, a man is flying!"

"What?" The Emperor stopped his fan.

"I saw him in the air, a man flying with wings. I heard a voice call out of the sky, and when I looked up, there he was, a dragon in the heavens with a man in its mouth, a dragon of paper and bamboo, colored like the sun and the grass."

"It is early," said the Emperor, "and you have just wakened from a dream."

"It is early, but I have seen what I have seen! Come, and you will see it too."

"Sit down with me here," said the Emperor. "Drink some tea. It must be a strange thing, if it is true, to see a man fly. You must have time to think of it, even as I must have time to prepare myself for the sight."

They drank tea.

"Please," said the servant at last, "or he will be gone."

The Emperor rose thoughtfully. "Now you may show me what you have seen."

They walked into a garden, across a meadow of grass, over a small bridge, through a grove of trees, and up a tiny hill.

"There!" said the servant.

The Emperor looked into the sky.

And in the sky, laughing so high that you could hardly hear him laugh, was a man; and the man was clothed in bright papers and reeds

2. **REREAD** Reread lines 5–37. Analyze the dialogue between the servant and the Emperor. What does the dialogue reveal about each character's feelings regarding the flying man?

to make wings and a beautiful yellow tail, and he was soaring all about like the largest bird in a universe of birds, like a new dragon in a land of ancient dragons.

The man called down to them from high in the cool winds of morning. "I fly, I fly!"

The servant waved to him. "Yes, *yes!*"

The Emperor Yuan did not move. Instead he looked at the Great Wall of China now taking shape out of the farthest mist in the green hills, that splendid snake of stones which **writhed** with majesty across the entire land. That wonderful wall which had protected them for a timeless time from enemy **hordes** and preserved peace for years without number. He saw the town, nestled to itself by a river and a road and a hill, beginning to waken.

writhed:

hordes:

"Tell me," he said to his servant, "has anyone else seen this flying man?"

"I am the only one, Excellency," said the servant, smiling at the sky, waving.

The Emperor watched the heavens another minute and then said, "Call him down to me."

"Ho, come down, come down! The Emperor wishes to see you!" called the servant, hands cupped to his shouting mouth.

The Emperor glanced in all directions while the flying man soared down the morning wind. He saw a farmer, early in his fields, watching the sky, and he noted where the farmer stood.

The flying man alit with a rustle of paper and a creak of bamboo reeds. He came proudly to the Emperor, clumsy in his rig, at last bowing before the old man.

"What have you done?" demanded the Emperor.

"I have flown in the sky, Your Excellency," replied the man.

"What *have* you done?" said the Emperor again.

"I have just told you!" cried the flier.

3. **READ ▶** As you read lines 46–103, continue to cite text evidence.

- Underline descriptions of the Great Wall of China in lines 46–52.
- In the margin, summarize what happens in lines 87–100.

"You have told me nothing at all." The Emperor reached out a thin hand to touch the pretty paper and the birdlike keel of the apparatus. It smelled cool, of the wind.

"Is it not beautiful, Excellency?"

"Yes, too beautiful."

"It is the only one in the world!" smiled the man. "And I am the inventor."

"The *only* one in the world?"

"I swear it!"

"Who else knows of this?"

"No one. Not even my wife, who would think me mad with the sun. She thought I was making a kite. I rose in the night and walked to the cliffs far away. And when the morning breezes blew and the sun rose, I gathered my courage, Excellency, and leaped from the cliff. I flew! But my wife does not know of it."

"Well for her, then," said the Emperor. "Come along."

They walked back to the great house. The sun was full in the sky now, and the smell of the grass was refreshing. The Emperor, the servant, and the flier paused within the huge garden.

The Emperor clapped his hands. "Ho, guards!"

The guards came running.

"Hold this man."

The guards seized the flier.

"Call the executioner," said the Emperor.

"What's this!" cried the flier, bewildered. "What have I done?" He began to weep, so that the beautiful paper apparatus rustled.

"Here is the man who has made a certain machine," said the Emperor, "and yet asks us what he has created. He does not know himself. It is only necessary that he create, without knowing why he has done so, or what this thing will do."

4. **◀ REREAD AND DISCUSS** Reread lines 64–100. With a small group, discuss the reason why the Emperor captured the flier. Cite text evidence in your discussion.

5. **READ ▶** As you read lines 104–150, continue to cite text evidence.

- Underline imagery that describes the Emperor's invention.
- Circle what the flier says he has done.
- In the margin, summarize the Emperor's concern.

The executioner came running with a sharp silver ax. He stood with his naked, large-muscled arms ready, his face covered with a **serene** white mask.

serene:

"One moment," said the Emperor. He turned to a nearby table upon which sat a machine that he himself had created. The Emperor took a tiny golden key from his own neck. He fitted his key to the tiny, delicate machine and wound it up. Then he set the machine going.

The machine was a garden of metal and jewels. Set in motion, the birds sang in tiny metal trees, wolves walked through miniature forests, and tiny people ran in and out of sun and shadow, fanning themselves with miniature fans, listening to tiny emerald birds, and standing by impossibly small but tinkling fountains.

"Is *it* not beautiful?" said the Emperor. "If you asked me what I have done here, I could answer you well. I have made birds sing, I have made forests murmur, I have set people to walking in this woodland, enjoying the leaves and shadows and songs. That is what I have done."

"But, oh, Emperor!" pleaded the flier, on his knees, the tears pouring down his face. "I have done a similar thing! I have found beauty. I have flown on the morning wind. I have looked down on all the sleeping houses and gardens. I have smelled the sea and even *seen* it, beyond the hills, from my high place. And I have soared like a bird; oh, I cannot say how beautiful it is up there, in the sky, with the wind about me, the wind blowing me here like a feather, there like a fan, the way the sky smells in the morning! And how free one feels! *That* is beautiful, Emperor, that is beautiful too!"

"Yes," said the Emperor sadly, "I know it must be true. For I felt my heart move with you in the air and I wondered: What is it like? How does it feel? How do the distant pools look from so high? And how my houses and servants? Like ants? And how the distant towns not yet awake?"

"Then spare me!"

"But there are times," said the Emperor, more sadly still, "when one must lose a little beauty if one is to keep what little beauty one already has. I do not fear you, yourself, but I fear another man."

"What man?"

"Some other man who, seeing you, will build a thing of bright papers and bamboo like this. But the other man will have an evil face and an evil heart, and the beauty will be gone. It is this man I fear."

"Why? Why?"

"Who is to say that someday just such a man, in just such an apparatus of paper and reed, might not fly in the sky and drop huge stones upon the Great Wall of China?" said the Emperor.

No one moved or said a word.

"Off with his head," said the Emperor.

The executioner whirled his silver ax.

"Burn the kite and the inventor's body and bury their ashes together," said the Emperor.

The servants retreated to obey.

The Emperor turned to his hand-servant, who had seen the man flying. "Hold your tongue. It was all a dream, a most sorrowful and beautiful dream. And that farmer in the distant field who also saw, tell him it would pay him to consider it only a vision. If ever the word passes around, you and the farmer die within the hour."

"You are merciful, Emperor."

"No, not merciful," said the old man. Beyond the garden wall he saw the guards burning the beautiful machine of paper and reeds that

6. **REREAD** Reread lines 109–144. Compare and contrast the two inventions in "The Flying Machine." Why does the Emperor only see beauty in his own creation? Cite textual evidence in your response.

7. **READ** As you read lines 151–174, continue to cite text evidence.

- In the margin, explain what the Emperor says in lines 151–155.
- Circle what the Emperor says in lines 160–163.
- Underline what the Emperor looks at in lines 164–172.

smelled of the morning wind. He saw he dark smoke climb into the sky. "No, only very much bewildered and afraid." He saw the guards digging a tiny pit wherein to bury the ashes. "What is the life of one man against those of a million others? I must take **solace** from that thought."

solace:

He took the key from its chain about his neck and once more wound up the beautiful miniature garden. He stood looking out across the land at the Great Wall, the peaceful town, the green fields, the rivers and streams. He sighed. The tiny garden whirred its hidden and delicate machinery and set itself in motion; tiny people walked in forests, tiny faces loped through sun-speckled glades in beautiful shining pelts, and among the tiny trees flew little bits of high song and bright blue and yellow colour, flying, flying, flying in that small sky.

"Oh," said the Emperor, closing his eyes, "look at the birds, look at the birds!"

8. **REREAD AND DISCUSS** Reread lines 173–174. With a small group, discuss your interpretation of the story's ending. What is the Emperor thinking about? Support your ideas with explicit textual evidence.

SHORT RESPONSE

Cite Text Evidence Recall that Bradbury says that he writes to warn people about dangers in the world around them. What warning is evident in "The Flying Machine"? **Cite text evidence** in your response.

1. **READ ▶** As you read the following two pages, begin to collect and cite text evidence.
   - Circle illustrations that show the characters' reactions to the "miracle."
   - Circle illustrations and text that tell you about the flying machine.
   - Circle the illustration of the Great Wall and explain its importance in the margin.

The FLYING MACHINE

2. **◀ REREAD** Contrast the drawings of the Emperor with the drawings of the servant. How do the illustrations convey each character's feelings about the flying machine?

THE EMPEROR GLANCED IN ALL DIRECTIONS WHILE THE FLYING MAN SOARED DOWN THE MORNING WIND. HE SAW A FARMER, EARLY IN HIS FIELDS, WATCHING THE SKY, AND HE NOTED WHERE THE FARMER STOOD...

THE FLYING MAN ALIT WITH A RUSTLE OF PAPER AND A CREAK OF BAMBOO REEDS. HE CAME PROUDLY TO THE EMPEROR, CLUMSY IN HIS RIG, AT LAST BOWING BEFORE THE OLD MAN...

THE EMPEROR REACHED OUT A THIN HAND TO TOUCH THE PRETTY PAPER AND THE BIRDLIKE KEEL OF THE APPARATUS. IT SMELLED COOL, OF THE WIND...

3. **READ ▶** As you read this page and the next, continue to cite text evidence.

- In the margin, explain the purpose of the Emperor's questions.
- On the next page, underline the question the flying man asks.
- Circle the close up of the Emperor's face.

4. **REREAD AND DISCUSS** In a small group, discuss how the Emperor's expression in the close-up image might affect your perception of the story. Cite textual evidence in your discussion.

THE MACHINE WAS A GARDEN OF METAL AND JEWELS. SET IN MOTION, BIRDS SANG IN TINY METAL TREES, WOLVES WALKED THROUGH MINIATURE FORESTS, AND TINY PEOPLE RAN IN AND OUT OF SUN AND SHADOW, FANNING THEMSELVES WITH MINIATURE FANS, LISTENING TO THE TINY EMERALD BIRDS, AND STANDING BY IMPOSSIBLY SMALL BUT TINKLING FOUNTAINS...

THE EMPEROR SAID...

THE FLIER, ON HIS KNEES, THE TEARS POURING DOWN HIS FACE, PLEADED...

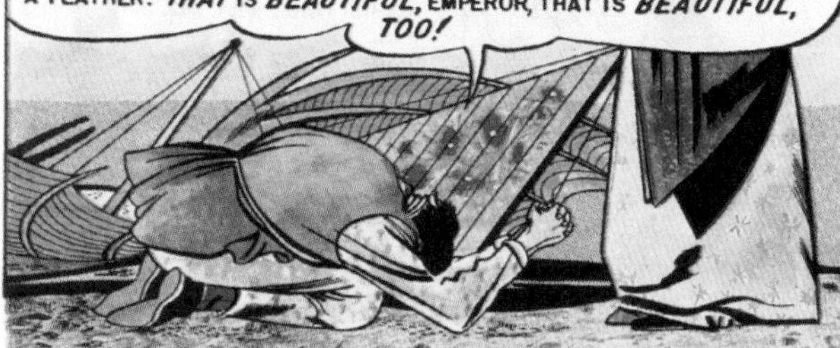

5. **READ ▶** As you read this page and the next, continue to cite text evidence.

- Circle repetitions of "beauty" and "beautiful," and in the margin, explain the flier's argument that his life should be spared.
- In the margin, explain the imagery that illustrates the flier's death.
- Circle birds in the last frame.

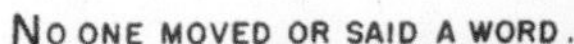
NO ONE MOVED OR SAID A WORD...

OFF WITH HIS HEAD!

THE EXECUTIONER WHIRLED HIS SILVER AX...

BURN THE KITE AND THE INVENTOR'S BODY AND BURY THEIR ASHES TOGETHER...
THE GUARDS RETREATED TO OBEY...

THE EMPEROR TURNED TO HIS SERVANT WHO HAD SEEN THE MAN FLYING...
HOLD YOUR TONGUE. IT WAS ALL A DREAM, A MOST SORROWFUL AND BEAUTIFUL DREAM. AND THAT FARMER IN THE DISTANT FIELD WHO ALSO SAW, TELL HIM IT WOULD PAY HIM TO CONSIDER IT ONLY A VISION. IF EVER THE WORD PASSES AROUND, YOU AND THE FARMER DIE WITHIN THE HOUR.
YOU ARE MERCIFUL EMPEROR.

THE OLD MAN SAW, BEYOND THE GARDEN WALL, THE GUARDS BURNING THE BEAUTIFUL MACHINE OF PAPER AND REEDS THAT SMELLED OF MORNING WIND. HE SAW THE DARK SMOKE CLIMB INTO THE SKY...
NO, NOT MERCIFUL. NO, ONLY VERY MUCH BEWILDERED AND AFRAID.

HE SAW THE GUARDS DIGGING A TINY PIT WHEREIN TO BURY THE ASHES...
WHAT IS THE LIFE OF ONE MAN AGAINST A MILLION OTHERS? I MUST TAKE SOLACE FROM THAT THOUGHT.

HE TOOK THE KEY FROM ITS CHAIN ABOUT HIS NECK AND ONCE MORE WOUND UP THE BEAUTIFUL MINATURE GARDEN. THE TINY GARDEN WHIRRED ITS HIDDEN AND DELICATE MACHINERY AND SET ITSELF INTO MOTION; TINY PEOPLE WALKED IN FORESTS, TINY FOXES LOPED THROUGH SUN-SPECKLED GLADES, AND AMONG THE TINY TREES FLEW LITTLE BITS OF HIGH SONG AND BRIGHT BLUE AND YELLOW COLOR, FLYING, FLYING, FLYING IN THAT SMALL SKY. AND THE EMPEROR SAID, CLOSING HIS EYES...
OH, LOOK AT THE BIRDS, LOOK AT THE BIRDS!
THE END
6

6. REREAD AND DISCUSS With a small group, discuss why the death of the flier was depicted as it was. What feelings might the writers have been trying to evoke by depicting his death this way? Cite text evidence in your discussion.

SHORT RESPONSE

Cite Text Evidence What are the advantages of reading "The Flying Machine" as a graphic story instead of a short story? Review your reading notes, and remember to **cite text evidence** in your response.

Background **Jim Haskins** *(1941–2005) was born into a large family in Demopolis, Alabama. After graduating from college, Haskins moved to New York City, where he taught special education classes in Harlem. He drew from his experiences there to write his first book,* Diary of a Harlem Schoolteacher. *Haskins's books for young adults often highlight the lives of famous African Americans, as well as African language and culture. A few of his books have been turned into movies, including the award-winning* The Cotton Club.

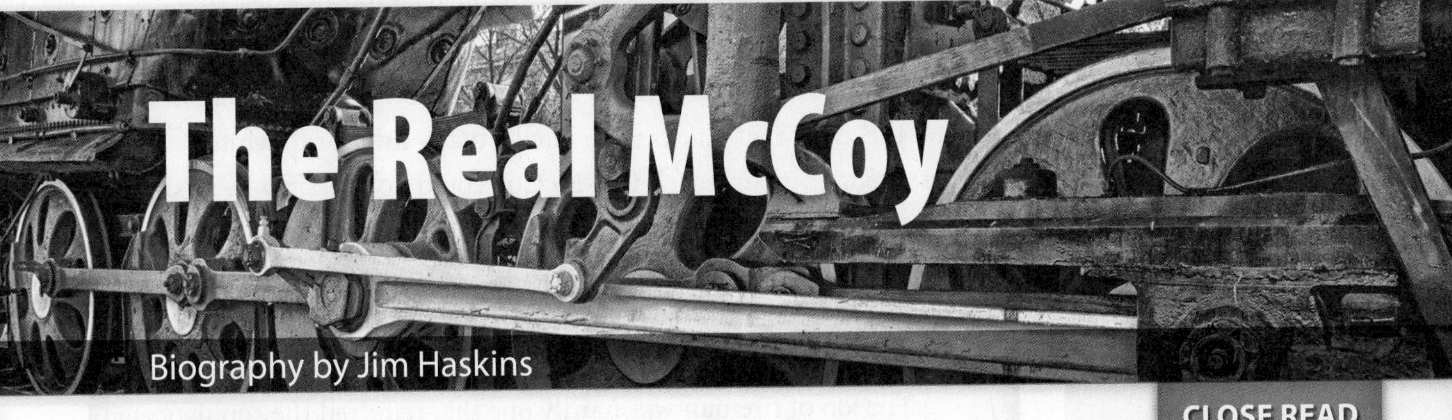

The Real McCoy

Biography by Jim Haskins

CLOSE READ Notes

1. **READ ▶** As you read lines 1–29, begin to collect and cite text evidence.
   - Underline details about the environment Elijah McCoy was born into and the different places where he lived.
   - Circle two sources of power during the age of the machine, and in the margin, explain why McCoy was fortunate to be born into that era.
   - In the margin, explain why McCoy could not get the kind of job he had been trained for.

Elijah McCoy's name is still remembered today and has become **synonymous** with the ideas of perfection and quality. When we say that something is "the real McCoy," we are remembering Elijah McCoy whether we are aware of it or not.

synonymous:

Elijah McCoy (1843–1929) was born on May 2, 1843, in Colchester, Ontario, Canada, the son of two runaway slaves, fugitives who had escaped from Kentucky by way of the Underground Railroad. After the Civil War, Elijah and his parents returned to the United States, settling down near Ypsilanti, Michigan. There Elijah attended school and worked in a machine shop.

McCoy, even as a boy, was fascinated with machines and tools. He was fortunate to have been born into an era that suited him perfectly, a time when newer and better machines were being invented—the age

of the machine. Following the footsteps of steam was that new energy source, electricity, which opened up even more opportunities for the inventive mind.

McCoy's interest only deepened with the emergence of each new device. He decided to go to Edinburgh, Scotland, where the bias against his color was not so evident, and serve an apprenticeship in mechanical engineering. After finishing his apprenticeship, McCoy returned to the United States a mechanical engineer, eager to put his skills to work. But companies at that time were reluctant to hire a black man to fill such a highly skilled position. Prejudice was strong and the myth that blacks were intellectually inferior to whites persisted. Companies felt that McCoy could not possibly be as skilled as he claimed to be and, even if he were, the white workers he might have to supervise would never take orders from a black man. The only job he was able to find was as a fireman on the Michigan Central Railroad.

The job of fireman was hardly one that required the sophisticated skills McCoy had obtained. His duties consisted of fueling the firebox of the engine to "keep the steam up" and oiling the engine. The way train and other types of engines were built meant that it was necessary to stop the train periodically—or to shut down whatever

2. **REREAD** Reread lines 1–29. What conclusions can you draw about each time McCoy changed his home? Support your answer with explicit textual evidence.

3. **READ** As you read lines 30–49, continue to cite textual evidence.

- Underline the words and images that describe a fireman's job.
- In the margin, explain what McCoy did to overcome "unthinking lethargy" (line 40).
- Circle what McCoy wanted to achieve.

"For two years he worked on the problem on his own time . . ."

engine was being used—so the moving parts could be lubricated. If the engines were not oiled, the parts would wear out quickly or friction would cause the parts to heat up, causing fires. Hand-lubricating engines was an inefficient but necessary procedure.

Many men or women, when faced with a repetitive, essentially mindless task, might sink into an unthinking **lethargy,** doing only that which is required of them and no more, but this was not true of Elijah McCoy. He did his job—oiling the engines—but that job led him to become interested in the problems of lubricating any kind of machinery that was in motion. For two years he worked on the problem on his own time in his own homemade machine shop. His

lethargy

4. REREAD Reread lines 31–38. Is there enough evidence to support the conclusion the author makes in lines 37–38? Support your response with explicit textual evidence.

initial idea was to manufacture the machines with canals cut into them with connecting devices between their various parts to distribute the oil throughout the machines while they were running. He wanted to make lubrication automatic.

Finally McCoy came up with what he called "the lubricating cup," or "drip cup." The lubricating cup was a small container filled with oil, with a stopcock to regulate the flow of oil into the parts of a moving machine. The lubricating or drip cup seemed an obvious invention, yet no one had thought of it before McCoy; it has since been described as the "key device in perfecting the overall lubrication system used in large industry today." With a drip cup installed, it was no longer necessary to shut down a machine in order to oil it, thus saving both time and money. McCoy received his patent for it on July 12, 1872.

5. READ ▶ As you read lines 50–72, continue to cite textual evidence.
- Circle the benefits of the "drip cup."
- In the margin, write why people would ask if a machine contained "the real McCoy."

6. ◀ REREAD Reread lines 50–59. What conclusions can you draw about why Elijah McCoy was the first to imagine the "drip cup," even though it seemed to be an "obvious invention"? Support your answer with explicit textual evidence.

The drip cup could be used on machinery of all types and it was quickly adopted by machine manufacturers everywhere. Of course, there were imitators, but their devices were not as effective or efficient as McCoy's. It soon became standard practice for an equipment buyer to inquire if the machine contained "the real McCoy." So commonly was this expression used that it soon spread outside the machine industry and came to have the general meaning of the "real thing," or perfection. Nowadays if someone states that they want "the real McCoy," it is taken to mean that they want the genuine article, the best, not a shoddy imitation. In 1872, of course, Elijah McCoy could not foresee that his name would soon become associated with the idea of perfection. All he knew was that the thing worked and worked well on machinery of all types.

The lubrication of machinery fascinated McCoy and he continued to work in that area. In 1892 he invented and patented a number of devices for lubricating locomotive engines. These inventions were used in all western railroads and on steamers plying the Great Lakes. Eventually McCoy would invent a total of twenty-three lubricators for different kinds of equipment and, in 1920, he applied his system to air brakes on vehicles.

During his lifetime, Elijah McCoy was awarded over fifty-seven patents and became known as one of the most prolific black inventors of the nineteenth century. In addition to his patents on various kinds of lubricating systems, he also received patents for such "homey" objects as an ironing table (a forerunner of today's ironing board), a lawn sprinkler, a steam dome and a dope cup (a cup for administering medicine). He eventually founded the Elijah McCoy Manufacturing Company in Detroit, Michigan, to develop and sell his inventions.

7. **READ ▶** As you read lines 73–92, continue to cite textual evidence.

- Underline McCoy's inventions.
- Circle a phrase that uses sensory details to appeal to the sense of hearing.
- In line 92, infer what "paean" means, and write your inference in the margin.

Until his death in 1929, McCoy continued working and inventing, sometimes patenting two or three new devices a year. Today, although many may not know who he was or what he did, his name remains to remind us of the idea of quality, and the steady, ceaseless roar of machinery is a paean to his inventiveness.

8. REREAD Reread lines 72–92. What conclusion can you make about why the author feels "the steady, ceaseless roar of machinery is a paean to" McCoy's "inventiveness"? Support your answer with explicit textual evidence.

SHORT RESPONSE

Cite Text Evidence What conclusions can you make about the way Elijah McCoy was treated after he invented the "drip cup"? Support your answer with **explicit textual evidence.**

Background *Regarding the topic of work, English humorist Jerome K. Jerome once wrote, "I like work: it fascinates me. I can sit and look at it for hours." As a testament to our frequent desire to avoid work, inventor Thomas Edison stated, "We often miss opportunity because it's dressed in overalls and looks like work." However, most people would agree that work adds value to our lives, and when we push ourselves to fulfill a particularly difficult task, we gain insight into what we can truly achieve.*

Poems About Work

To Be of Use . . . . Marge Piercy

A Story of How a Wall Stands. . . . . . Simon J. Ortiz

Marge Piercy *(b. 1936) was born into a family that struggled against the effects of the Great Depression. Her love of literature was instilled at a young age when she came down with rheumatic fever and was only able to read to entertain herself. The novels and poetry she writes frequently deal with the topics of feminism and social change. One of her most famous novels,* Women on the Edge of Time, *even incorporates elements of time travel.*

Simon J. Ortiz *(b. 1941) is one of the most influential and widely read American Indian writers. Ortiz was raised in Acoma Pueblo reservation as part of the Eagle Clan, where he spoke only his native language. When he was sent to boarding school, he was encouraged to speak English, and his struggle in transitioning between two different cultures led him to write about his experiences. Later, he would write as a means to bring attention to the American Indian voice, a voice he felt was unrepresented in American literature.*

1. READ ▶ As you read "To Be of Use," cite text evidence.
   - Underline metaphors in lines 1–11.
   - In the margin, summarize the people the speaker admires.

To Be of Use

by Marge Piercy

The people I love the best
jump into work head first
without dallying in the shallows
and swim off with sure strokes almost out of sight.
They seem to become natives of that element,
the black sleek heads of seals
bouncing like half-submerged balls.

I love people who harness themselves, an ox to a heavy cart,
who pull like water buffalo, with massive patience,
who strain in the mud and the muck to move things forward,
who do what has to be done, again and again.

I want to be with people who submerge
in the task, who go into the fields to harvest
and work in a row and pass the bags along,
who are not parlor generals and field deserters
but move in a common rhythm
when the food must come in or the fire be put out.

The work of the world is common as mud.
Botched, it smears the hands, crumbles to dust.
But the thing worth doing well done
has a shape that satisfies, clean and evident.
Greek amphoras for wine or oil,
Hopi vases that held corn, are put in museums
but you know they were made to be used.
The pitcher cries for water to carry
and a person for work that is real.

2. ◀ REREAD AND DISCUSS Reread lines 18–26. In a small group, discuss what the author means by "The work of the world is common as mud." What idea does she emphasize by personifying the pitcher?

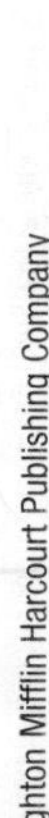

3. READ ▶ As you read "A Story of How a Wall Stands," begin to collect and cite text evidence.

- In the margin, explain what the speaker of "To Be of Use" would most likely admire about the father in this poem.
- Circle phrases that are repeated.

A Story of How a Wall Stands

by Simon J. Ortiz

My father, who works with stone,
says, "That's just the part you see,
the stones which seem to be
just packed in on the outside,"
and with his hands puts the stone and mud
in place. "Underneath what looks like loose stone,
there is stone woven together."
He ties one hand over the other,
fitting like the bones of his hands
and fingers. "That's what is
holding it together."

"It is built that carefully,"
he says, "the mud mixed
to a certain texture," patiently
"with the fingers," worked
in the palm of his hand. "So that
placed between the stones, they hold
together for a long, long time."

He tells me those things,
the story of them worked
with his fingers, in the palm
of his hands, working the stone
and the mud until they become
the wall that stands a long, long time.

4. REREAD Reread lines 12–24. What is the effect of the author's use of repetition? Support your answer with explicit textual evidence.

SHORT RESPONSE

Cite Text Evidence Why do you think the poets chose to write these poems in free verse? What effect does the free verse structure have on the reader? Review your reading notes, and be sure to **cite evidence from the text** in your response.

Acknowledgments

Excerpt from "Civil War Journal" from *The Journals of Louisa May Alcott* by Louisa May Alcott, edited by Joel Myerson, Daniel Shealy, and Madeleine B. Stern. Text copyright © 1989 by The Estate of Theresa W. Pratt. Reprinted by permission of Joel Myerson.

Excerpt from *The Diary of Anne Frank* by Frances Goodrich and Albert Hackett. Text copyright © 1956 by Albert Hackett, Frances Goodrich Hackett, and Otto Frank. Reprinted by permission of Random House, Inc. Any third party use of this material, outside of this publication, is prohibited. Interested parties must apply directly to Random House, Inc. for permission.

"The Flying Machine" from *The Ray Bradbury Chronicles: Volume Two* by Ray Bradbury. Text copyright © 1992 by Ray Bradbury. Illustrations copyright © 1954 by Fables Publishing Co., Inc. © renewed 1982 William M. Gaines, Agent. Illustrations used by agreement with J. Boylston & Company, Publishers. Reprinted with permission of Brick Tower Press, Inc. Text reprinted by permission of Don Congdon Associates, Inc.

"The Flying Machine" by Ray Bradbury, from *Golden Apples of the Sun.* Text copyright © 1953, renewed 1981 by Ray Bradbury. Reprinted by permission of Don Congdon Associates, Inc.

"Frankenstein" from *Counting Myself Lucky: Selected Poems 1963-1992* by Edward Field. Text copyright © 1992 by Edward Field. Reprinted by permission of Black Sparrow Press, an imprint of David R. Godine, Publisher, Inc.

"Golden Glass" by Alma Luz Villanueva from *Hispanics in the U.S.: An Anthology of Creative Literature edited* by Francisco Jimenez and Gary D. Keller. Text copyright © 1981 by Alma Luz Villanueva. Reprinted by permission of Bilingual Press/Editorial Bilingue, Arizona State University.

"Hard on the Gas" from *Behind the Wheel: Poems About Driving* by Janet S. Wong. Text copyright © 1999 by Janet S. Wong. Reprinted by permission of Janet S. Wong.

"Identity" by Julio Noboa Polanco. Text copyright © 1962 by Julio Noboa Polanco. Reprinted by permission of Julio Noboa Polanco.

Excerpt from "Man-Made Monsters" from *A Natural History of Unnatural Things* by Daniel Cohen. Text copyright © 1971 by Daniel Cohen. Reprinted by permission of Henry Morrison, Inc. on behalf of Daniel Cohen.

"Museum Indians," from *Roofwalker* by Susan Power. Text copyright © 2002 by Susan Power. Reprinted by permission of Milkweed Editions and the Dunow, Carlson & Lerner Literary Agency on behalf of Susan Power.

"My Friend Douglass" from *Abraham Lincoln & Frederick Douglass* by Russell Freedman. Text copyright © 2012 by Russell Freedman. Reprinted by permission of Houghton Mifflin Harcourt Publishing Company.

"The Outsider" from *H.P. Lovecraft Tales* by H.P. Lovecraft. Text copyright © by H.P. Lovecraft. Reprinted by permission of Jabberwocky Literary Agency.

"The Real McCoy" from *Outward Dreams: Black Inventors and Their Inventions* by Jim Haskins. Text copyright © 1991 by Jim Haskins. Reprinted by permission of Walker and Company.

"A Story of How a Wall Stands" from *Woven Stone* by Simon J. Ortiz. Published by University of Arizona Press, Tucson, AZ. Text copyright © 1992 by Simon J. Ortiz. Reprinted by permission of Simon J. Ortiz.

"To Be of Use" from *Circles on the Water* by Marge Piercy. Text copyright © 1973, 1982 by Marge Piercy and Middlemarsh, Inc. Reprinted by permission of Alfred A. Knopf, a division of Random House, Inc. and Wallace Literary Agency, Inc. Any third party use of this material, outside of this publication, is prohibited. Interested parties must apply directly to Random House, Inc. for permission.

"The Whistle" from *Down Garrapata Road* by Anne Estevis. Text copyright © 2003 by Anne Estevis. Reprinted by permission of Arte Público Press - University of Houston.

Index of Titles & Authors